Tsvi Bisk

THE SUICIDE OF THE JEWS
A Cautionary Tale

Tsvi Bisk

THE SUICIDE OF THE JEWS

A Cautionary Tale

Senior Editors & Producers: Contento
Editor: Lindy Kawalsky
Design: Liliya Lev Ari
Cover Design: Benjie Herskowitz

ISBN: 978-965-550-486-6

International sole distributor: Contento
22 Isserles Street, 6701457 Tel Aviv, Israel

www.ContentoNow.com
netanel@contento-publishing.com

Tsvi Bisk

THE SUICIDE OF THE JEWS
A Cautionary Tale

Table of Contents:

For Micaela
The best friend anyone could have

Acknowledgements

This book is the third of a trilogy. The first was *Futurizing the Jews* (Praeger, 2003) co-authored with my friend and colleague Dr. Rabbi Moshe Dror. The book was my intellectual biography and a summation of 30 years of thinking and writing about the paramount importance of futurist thinking for the survival of the Jewish People. The second was *The Optimistic Jew* (Maxanna Press, 2007) which attempted to present a positive vision for the Jewish People in the 21st century. *The Suicide of the Jews* is a cautionary tale of how resentment has caused Israel to pursue policies that are more dangerous to the future survival of the Jewish people than any external enemy.

As my dedication indicates the driving force behind me on this project has been my wife and best friend Micaela Ziv. Without her support and encouragement I would not have completed this work.

In writing the book the faces of my four children – Yonit, Dori, Nati and Mor – were constantly before me. What kind of future were I and my generation bequeathing to them? What would be the nature of the communal identity we would be remembered for? All parents who love their children are futurists. My love for my children provided me with the energy to stick with the project. It goes without saying that there would be no book without my late parents Max and Anne. I am increasingly aware of what part of them is in me and how I am the product of their character and fortitude.

I must also acknowledge the place that the Nessyahu family played in my life. Everything I am intellectually, as a Jew and as a Zionist is a result of my being "adopted" by them when I came to Israel. Mordechai, Yehudit and Haimie are all deceased now and this has left a hole in my life.

The Author's Worldview

To be coherent and clear, an essay or a book must have a transparent starting point. Who I am and what I have become is my starting point. I was born and educated in America and came to Israel in my early 20's – one day before the 6 Day War. I became a Zionist not because of ideological conviction but because I fell in love with Israel and the potential of its people. My motivations for writing the book as well as the views expressed in it are derived from an intense feeling that there is something exceptional about Jewish peoplehood; that we betray our ancestors, ourselves and human history when we turn our backs on that exceptionality. I believe that the modern State of Israel is not only a framework to guarantee the physical survival of the Jewish people; it is also a vessel by which we can give modern expression to the energy, idealism and creativity that has characterized so much of Jewish history. I also believe that unless we strive to achieve this second aspect of Israel's mission we will not succeed in sustaining the first and thus will not survive.

The book is a manifestation of a wider Jewish and Zionist vision which asserts that: *If Israel will not be a light unto the nations it will not be a light unto the Jews* and thus will have no reason to survive. This was a view held by David Ben Gurion. It is also my view.

Please visit my blog

www.tsvibisk.com

In order to: learn about my lectures, workshops and seminars for missions in Israel, events in your communities and organizational conventions.

Foreword

"To accept tradition without examining it with intelligence and judgment is like the blind blindly following others"

Bahya Ibn Paquda (11th century Rabbi and ethical philosopher):
Duties of the Heart

"...only decadent peoples, on the way down, feel an urgent need to mythologize and live in their past. A vigorous people, on the way up, is more concerned with visions of its future..."

Arthur Lewis, African American Nobel Prize winner in Economics

There are two fundamental visions regarding the essence of Zionism. One says that the purpose of Zionism is to redeem the past; that the Jewish people are obligated by history to create a state in order to redeem the *entire* Land of Israel (which would include Judea, Samaria, and parts of Lebanon, Syria and Jordan). This vision sees the state as a means to the land and the people as a means to the state. The land becomes a *Moloch* – a pagan god that is idolatrized and worshiped.

Jewish history becomes a dictator of Jewish behavior. This vision has been in ascendance since the 6-Day War.

The second vision says the purpose of Zionism is to create alternative future options for the Jews by creating one state on the planet in which the Jews are a majority. This vision sees the land as the means to the state and the state as the means to serve the people. It sees the land as an essential prerequisite for the creation of the state and the state as an essential prerequisite for creating alternative future options for the Jewish people. It sees Jewish history as an inspiration for the Jewish people, not its dictator. Inspiration is also a means – without pride, honor and self-esteem it is impossible to mobilize the energy and focus to undertake and realize heroic historical tasks, and the creation of Israel is nothing if not a heroic historical achievement. Thus, the Jewish state being created *within* a portion of the historical land of Israel (not necessarily throughout the *entire* land of Israel) rather than elsewhere, was an essential prerequisite and a necessary means to the ultimate end of creating alternative possible future options for the Jewish people. This is the vision I embrace but which has been in decline since the 6-Day War. The decline of my vision of Zionism and the ascendance of the land-fetishism vision terrifies me and makes me fearful about the future survival of the Jewish people.

Because of this, I have come to conclude that the ideological settlement project, and even more importantly, the settler's cultural influence throughout the country, is more dangerous to the survival of Israel than the Iranian nuclear program. I increasingly see the direction Israel is taking as being suicidal. To paraphrase Lincoln, Israel cannot for long exist half democratic (the constitutional democracy in which *all* Israel's citizens live) and half undemocratic (the military regime in the West Bank). It must eventually become one or the other but it cannot be both. Either the regime in the West Bank becomes democratic (which means the end of Israel as a Jewish state) or the regime in Israel proper will become increasingly undemocratic.

I do not want to mislead the reader. I have little sympathy for the Palestinians. After their rejection of Ehud Barak's proposals at Camp David in 2000 and the second intifada I have concluded that the Palestinians hate the Jews more than they love themselves, while the Jews love themselves more than they hate the Palestinians. This is a fundamental asymmetry that the politically correct left has trouble accommodating within their postmodern moral relativism, but it is nonetheless self-evident for anyone with eyes to see and a brain to think.

At Camp David in 2000, 60% of Israeli Jews supported Ehud Barak's plan to give 95% of the West Bank and Gaza to the Palestinians with matching land swaps of Israeli state land to make up for the remaining 5%. This plan also offered East Jerusalem as the capital of the Palestinian state. This offer was dismissively rejected and Arafat began planning the second intifada. Arik Sharon's 'visit' to the Temple Mount had nothing to do with it, as Arafat's wife Suha eventually confirmed. Subsequent proposals by Israeli leaders such as Ehud Olmert were even more generous and were also rejected dismissively. To my dismay, I have come to agree with Israel's political right: that the ultimate aim of the Palestinians is still the destruction of Israel (as silly as this might sound to a rational person) and that this takes precedence over the creation of a state of their own. Where I disagree with the Right is that this fact does not obligate the Jews to be as stupid as the Palestinians and thus pursue a policy that ultimately will lead to the destruction of Israel and the enfeebling of the Diaspora.

The Right thinks it can get away with maintaining the present half free/half 'slave' situation; the Left believes that if only Israel were really nice to the well-meaning Palestinians we would have peace, the lamb would lay down with the lion and Arab and Jew could walk hand in hand singing *We Shall Overcome* as they tiptoe through the tulips of universal brotherhood. I believe that the Left and the Right are both guilty of self-deception on a colossal scale, but I believe the policies of the Right are more dangerous to the survival of the state than the Left, that the Right has come to the wrong conclusions for the right reasons and that the Left has come to the right conclusions for the wrong reasons. The following, therefore, is a cautionary tale about the future; about what *might* be the fate of the Jewish People unless we change our ways. It is an 'imagineered' history written from the future perspective of 2099. I have borrowed this device from *Old-New-Land* by Theodore Herzl (the founder of modern political Zionism) and from Edward Bellamy's 19th century classic *Looking Backward: From 2000 to 1887*. The fictitious author is writing a book entitled *The Decline and Fall of Israel and the Jewish People*. The following is his working draft of his analysis of the developments that led to the end of the Jewish People.

The Decline & Fall of Israel
& the Jewish People

by Howard Mathewson (2099)

Introduction

Perhaps the Israeli-Palestinian conflict should have been renamed "Dumb & Dumber". For the first 65 years of Israel's existence the Jews were dumb but the Palestinians were dumber; or as Abba Eban so aptly put it, the Palestinians "never missed an opportunity to miss an opportunity".

But by 2012 a change of roles had become apparent. It was not an overnight change, but one that had been developing for some time. The Jews had gradually but decisively become the dumber in this equation. Israeli political thinking had degenerated into slogans, with no room for nuanced thinking. Stupidity had become a virtue as long as it was clothed in the manly rhetoric of 'tough-minded thinking'. This led to the collapse of Israel and as a consequence the rapid erosion of the Diaspora into eventual extinction. The question that has bothered many researchers is: "How could the smartest people in the world make the dumbest decisions in the world and destroy themselves"?

The very question has racialist undertones that disturb many liberal advocates of politically correct ethnic equality. Yet few would have denied that the modern European anti-Semitism of the 19th and 20th centuries stemmed, to a certain extent, from fear of the Jews' perceived intelligence. Even Adolf Eichmann said: "...we are fighting an enemy who... is intellectually superior to us"[1]. Throughout European history, the Jews were viewed as being shrewder and cleverer than other people, and therefore non-Jews should be careful in their dealings with them. Jews were resented for using this perceived intelligence unfairly and becoming disproportionately represented in the free professions and business; 'dominating', as it were, national economic and cultural life. Jews were seen as dispossessing the native ethnic group – the *"authentic"* nation. Anti-Semitism as an ideology and as a movement was in many ways a defense mechanism of non-Jews against the perceived 'scheming' brainpower of the Jews. Zionism, as the national liberation movement of the Jewish people, subsequently became the Jewish defense mechanism against this anti-Semitism.

This populist perception of Jewish brainpower was not entirely groundless. Empirical evidence seemed to bear it out. In countries with a constitutionalist legal foundation (those countries that following the Enlightenment enabled the Jews to operate as freely as other citizens), the percentage of Jews rising to the top of society in business and the free professions was out of all proportion to their numbers in society. By 2012, 22% of all Nobel Prize laureates had been Jewish, (27% in physics and 31% in medicine). These percentages had been so disproportionate to the percentage of Jews in the world's population (1/5th of 1%) as to be statistically implausible. Jewish achievements in the United States, the most constitutionalist and mobile country the world had ever known, were even more impressive. In 2012 Jews constituted 2% of the U.S. population, but 21% of the Ivy League student bodies, 37% of the Academy Award-winning directors, and 51% of the Pulitzer Prize winners for nonfiction.

The Jewish State was not far behind the Diaspora in its intellectual achievements. Israel had more high-tech start-ups per capita than any other nation. It led the world in civilian R&D spending per capita. It was second behind the U.S. in the number of companies listed on the NASDAQ (ahead of Japan, Germany, France, England, China and India). Israel, with only eight million people, attracted as much venture capital as France and Germany combined.

The qualitative gap between Israel and her Arab neighbors was enormous. From 1980 to 2000, Egyptians registered 77 patents in the U.S.; Saudis registered 171, while Israelis registered 7,652. All told, by 2012 Israel had recorded 16,805 patents in its history, while the entire Arab League (with a population of about 350,000,000) had recorded about 836 patents in total. In 2008 alone, Israel registered 1166 patents, more than all Arab states had done in their entire history. (Arab League countries registered 71 patents in 2008). Israeli superiority in the field of science and technology compared to all the Arab countries combined was indisputable. Three Israeli universities were listed in the top 100 in the world by international classifications; all seven Israeli research universities were ranked in the top 500. No university in the entire Arab League was listed in the top five hundred. Israel spent twice as much on scientific research as the entire Arab world, 4.7% of its national output was dedicated to research; the highest proportion of spending in the world. Arab countries, on the other hand, spent only 0.2% of their national income on research.

Fashionable 'enlightened' thinking held that this Jewish intellectual predominance was attributable *solely* to their unique historical, cultural and sociological background, not to any inherent 'genetic' disposition. Following the horrors of WWII, 'inherent' explanations were viewed as racialist and thus dangerous. Jews especially shied away from it like the plague. But within several decades after WWII, less fearful researchers asked if this unique *subjective* historical, cultural and sociological background had not indeed favored higher intelligence in an *objective* evolutionary way and thus had created a greater 'genetic' tendency to higher median intelligence. Not surprisingly the question was first publically addressed in 1969 by the conservative *non-Jewish* sociologist Ernest Van den Haag in his bestselling book *The Jewish Mystique*. No self-respecting politically-left researcher would have dared to even ask such a racialist question and the Jews were terrified of public discussion on this issue (even though in private they *implicitly* acknowledged it by way of the Yiddish synonym for stupidity – a 'goyishe kop' which literally means a gentile brain, which implies stupidity).

In 2009, Dr. Gregory Cochran (physicist and anthropologist) and Prof. Henry Harpending (anthropologist), both non-Jews, published *The 10,000 Year Explosion*[2] which claimed significant genetic mutations could take place in very short evolutionary time (hundreds of years) and that amongst other things this explained the significantly higher median IQ of Ashkenazi Jews. The final chapter in their book was entitled "Medieval Evolution: How the Ashkenazi Jews Got their Smarts", which described how the discriminatory life style imposed on the Jews in medieval Europe favored the survival of Jewish individuals with a propensity for abstract thinking and imagination. In 2011, independent researcher Hank Pellissier (another non-Jew) published *Why is the IQ of Ashkenazi Jews so High?*[3] In this book he evangelized the Jewish intellectual lifestyle as a way to raise the IQ of the entire human race – making the Jews a kind of genetic "Light unto the Gentiles". No Jew, of course, would have dared make such claims.

So how is it that the so-called 'smartest people in the world', when finally attaining autonomous political power after 2,000 years, began to worship the land and as a consequence acted so stupidly that they essentially killed themselves? One Jewish wit, listing the achievements of Zionism (revivifying the Hebrew Language, greening the desert, creating Silicon Wadi etc.), added "finally dispelling the racist canard that Jews were smarter than other people; give us political power and we are just as stupid as everyone else". Comparative linguistics might provide a clue. In Hebrew there is no word for intelligence that signifies brute quantitative brainpower; the thing that IQ tests measure. Thus Modern Hebrew invented *intelligenti* (a Hebraization of the English) when signifying brute quantitative brainpower (IQ). The word for stupid in Hebrew is *'tipesh'* which is not the opposite of intelligent but rather the opposite of wise, or *'chacham'*. In Hebrew people can be both very intelligent and very stupid. (This of course sounds like a description of politicians and academics worldwide, whatever their ethnicity.) This begs the question; if the Jews had only followed the inherent wisdom of their own language, might they still exist as a small but vital community contributing disproportionately to human civilization. This is an instructive linguistic inkling for the tragic tale that follows: first the death of Israel followed by the withering of the Jewish Diaspora.

Israel died in 2048 with an internal cancerous whimper; not from an external nuclear bang. It was not the fanatic racist hatred of the Iranian thug government, or the vile anti-Semitism of the Arab world, or the 'Liberation Struggle' of the Palestinians, or the acknowledged double standard of the European Left that killed Israel, but rather decades of poor 'life-style' choices: of grand-strategic stupidity, overweening arrogance, illogical responses to real threats and provocations, and paranoid responses to perceived threats and provocations. But most of all, from losing its historic way and setting up false gods to worship: from being activist in areas it had no business being activist in, thus inhibiting activism in areas it should have been activist in. The idolatry of the *Land of Israel* had become the cancer of Zionist activity, consuming hugely disproportionate amounts of energy, attention, and treasure.

I use the term poor 'life-style' choices because Israel's political and religious classes came to resemble a 'three pack a day smoker' who thought he could jog every day; who thought the laws of statistical probability did not apply to him because he prayed to the true God by means of the 'true' religion. Israel was 'special' (chosen) and thus immune to the constraints of global geopolitics and could allow itself to be indifferent to the ambitions of its own university-trained young people who wished to participate in the exciting opportunities of the global economy of the 21st century. Such ambitions were seen as egoistic self-indulgence in contrast to the heroic idealism of the settlers and thus not worthy of respect. Like the three pack a day smoker, Israel finally gave itself the political, economic and cultural cancer that killed it.

One of the noblest endeavors in human history, a story of unsurpassed idealism, heroism, invention and imagination – the story of a people oppressed like no other in history, rising from the ashes of the greatest crime in history – the story of a country that in its infancy inspired the entire world with its achievements in the face of overwhelming odds, slid whimpering into history in 2048, exactly one hundred years after its founding. Its initial successes having gone to its head, it was defeated by its misjudgments, it came to believe that it was capable of doing anything it wished without any negative consequences; it was done in by ignoring the constraints of reality. This second tragedy, equal in its terrible consequences to the Holocaust, literally killed Diaspora Jewry. The Diaspora, like a parent that had lost a second child, lost the will to live as a communal and cultural collective, and within a decade after the death of Israel all its major institutions had collapsed and only a tiny remnant, here and there, made any effort to sustain themselves as Jews. The following is the story of 100 years of heroic futility.

Part I – Background

*H*istory matters! Every success and every failure has numerous historical roots. In order to understand how the "smartest" people in the world made the dumbest decisions and destroyed themselves, we have to examine the historical developments that molded their mentality and provided the psychological framework for their decision making. The following chapters attempt to describe the multi-faceted background that created this self-destructive frame of mind.

Chapter One

The Evolution of Jewish Identity

Zionism was the most recent iteration of the ever-changing character of Jewish identity. Identity is evolutionary for every people. To be English today is different from being English in the time of Queen Victoria, Elizabeth I, or Alfred the Great. Similarly, being Jewish in 2020 was different from being Jewish a hundred years before, five hundred years before, or two thousand years before. Modern Jewish identity was a consequence of thousands of years of cultural evolution from The Fathers (Abraham, Isaac and Jacob), to the Judges, to the Kings, to the Prophets, to the Sadducees, to the Pharisees, to the Exile and Rabbinic Judaism, up to the Scientific Revolution and the Emancipation, and the subsequent pluralism that derived from the European Enlightenment.

The most significant post-Enlightenment development for the Jews was the shift from a primarily religious identity to a primarily ethnic or national identity[4]. The Enlightenment gave birth to human agency as a cultural value: active messianism replaced passive messianism. What we call *The Idea of Progress* produced political ideologies dedicated to changing society for the betterment of all people and every person. In the American *Declaration of Independence*, Thomas Jefferson best expressed the idea that the betterment of the people is the *only* purpose of government and that government is *only* legitimate when it serves the will, needs and wishes of the people.

> We hold these truths to be self-evident, that all men are created equal that they are endowed by their Creator with certain unalienable Rights, that among these are Life, Liberty and the pursuit of Happiness. *That to secure these rights, Governments are instituted among Men,* (italics mine) deriving their just powers from the consent of the governed

When the Enlightenment transformed Jewish identity from religious to ethnic, it gave birth to the yearning for national self-determination which gave birth to Zionism. At first the Enlightenment diluted Jewish attachment to the old unifying religious forms, creating divisions. Ironically the ethnic and romantic nationalisms which were born out of the Enlightenment inspired modern anti-Semitism as well as Zionism as the response to anti-Semitism. Nationalism became manifest in nation-states which found the presence of a large minority of Jews, with customs and religion different from the majority 'authentic' nation, disconcerting if not intolerable. Paradoxically, emancipation made the Jewish problem more rather than less acute. Unless they assimilated, Jews were seen as alien growths in the healthy body of the authentic nation; yet Jews who did assimilate were viewed with no less suspicion. T.S. Eliot, that personification of the urbane anti-Semite, expressed the opinion that too many Jews of 'that sort' (assimilationist) were undesirable as they, by the very nature of striving to be part of the 'authentic' nation, upset social stability and cultural uniformity. In his book *After Strange Gods* he wrote:

> The population should be homogeneous; where two or more cultures exist in the same place they are likely either to be fiercely self-conscious or both to become adulterate. What is still more important is unity of religious background, and reasons of race and religion combine to make any large number of *free-thinking* (italics mine) Jews undesirable.[5]

Free-thinking Jews bothered Eliot more than Orthodox Jews, who tended to ghettoize themselves and thus not "adulterate" the authentic culture. The double irony was that Zionism and the creation of Israel as a nation-state trying to be part of a world community of nation states became an outlier at its very birth, and was seen by many in the world community to be an artificial invention and not an "authentic" national entity, not a true colleague of the other "authentic" nation states. Anti-Zionism eventually became the new (postmodern) anti-Semitism. This manifested itself in the postmodernist claim that Jewish identity per se was but an artificial construct (since it did not fit into the neat anthropological, sociological or theological definitions favored by academia). From this, Zionism and Jewish attachment to the Land of Israel were also constructs (artificial inventions) and thus undeserving of respect as compelling ethical positions.

But this view could very well have been defined as a philosophical *Bill of Attainder*[6] because when analyzed, all modern identity had been invented: Bismarck invented Germany; Mazzini and Garibaldi invented Italy and the Founding Fathers invented the United States of America. By the year 2000, over half the member states of the United Nations were invented out of the postcolonial experience – including almost every Muslim country (Iran and Egypt being the exceptions). A case could be made that modern English identity was invented by an Italian Jew (Disraeli) defending a German Queen (Victoria) in the name of "our ancient English traditions rooted in the mists of time". Israel's indignant reaction to this global double standard resulted in a political psychology that led to irrational decisions which contributed to its eventual demise.

Identity as an ongoing evolutionary/reinvention process was especially applicable to the Jews. A normative, restricted definition of what it meant to be Jewish became impossible after the Enlightenment: was Jewish identity a religion, a nationality, an ethnic group, or a civilization. Even the Jews could not agree. A famous Jewish joke of the time was that a Jew could be defined as somebody who constantly asked the question "who is a Jew?" This self-identity confusion complicated the world's attitude to Israel. The Jews had become an ideologically and culturally pluralistic people.

Ideologically, Jewish religious identity included ultra-Orthodox, modern Orthodox, Conservative, Reform, Reconstructionist, Humanist and trans-denominational Judaism. Jewish ethnic identity also included secular atheists and agnostics, such as some of the greatest Jews of modern times: Einstein, Freud, Herzl, Ben Gurion, Weizmann, and Jabotinsky. Even prior to the Enlightenment, Jewish identity had been modified by the non-Jewish cultures the Jews had lived in. These Jewish identities included Ashkenazi, Sephardic and Middle Eastern which further subdivided into German, Yemenite, Russian, Iraqi, Moroccan and American Jews. The only universal norms of Jewish identity were the prohibition against idolatry and the requirement of unqualified individual responsibility. Judaism was an 'ism' – an ideology about life that *contained* a religious tradition. It was a tradition and a worldview dependent on individual behavior. It had little place for the vicarious 'salvation' inherent in the principle of grace or 'right belief.' Jews were instructed to be 'partners with God' in the ongoing act of creation; it was an active, not a passive belief system – you had to *do* things, not just pray.

In a way, this pre-Enlightenment attitude was kind of a proto human-agency mindset that rewarded human energy and might have explained the tremendous achievements of Jews in the 19th and 20th centuries better than the doubtful genetic explanations offered above. It might have also been an explanation for disproportionate Jewish involvement in the great reformist political and social movements of the 19th and 20th centuries; changing society for the better found a natural home in a mindset conditioned by a culture that advocated "being a partner with God in the act of creation". The way one behaved (*Derech Eretz*) was always fundamental to Jewishness, not one's ideological belief system. The hijacking of Jewish tradition by a politicized right-wing religious establishment dedicated to land idolatry and presenting itself as "authentic" Judaism alienated many Israelis and Diaspora Jews from Jewish religious tradition and eventually from its quintessential secular expression – Zionism. This caused an ongoing de-vitalization of Jewish identity both in Israel and in the Diaspora. This eventually resulted in weakened Jewish communal life and support for Israel in the Diaspora.

The test for Jewish survival had always been empirical. If a form of Judaism endured, it was because it had contributed something of value to a critical mass of Jewish individuals, not because it had some inherent abstract theoretical value. It was the spiritual equivalent of the survival of the fittest. What survived did so because it answered a need and gave value to real human beings. Culture, after all, is not a museum dedicated to preserving artifacts from the past, nor is it a cemetery dedicated to eulogizing the heroes of the past. It is a dynamic, future-oriented creative process; it is a living thing that evolves as a consequence of its dynamic interaction with other cultures and other cultural environments. What does not interact does not evolve; what does not evolve dies.

The land idolatry and culture of self-righteous indignation that characterized the latter stages of the Zionist project eventually drove ever growing numbers of Israelis into a culturally isolationist frame of mind. Israelis took pride in being a people who dwelt alone; took pride in not taking evolving global values into account, and saw this indifference to global attitudes as a badge of Jewish authenticity. Zionism became inert; it ceased to interact with other cultures. Thus it was that Zionism, as the last stage of Jewish identity, eventually failed the empirical test and took the entire Jewish people down with it.

Chapter Two

The European Roots of Modern Zionism

The *Zionist Idea* in its modern formulation was a product of 17th, 18th and 19th century European developments, primarily the Scientific Revolution, the Enlightenment and the Industrial Revolution. By introducing the idea of human agency as the driving force of organized society these developments gave birth to *The Idea of Progress*. The products of *The Idea of Progress* included the American and French Revolutions, the Industrial Revolution, Liberalism, Socialism and social reform movements, as well as Marxism and Nationalism.

Zionism was constituted from and influenced by all of these. The concept of active agency – to take ones fate into one's own hands – was the foundational driver of the *Zionist Idea* and flouted the traditional passive religious view that the

Jews will be restored to their historical homeland when the Messiah comes. But human agency is not just an abstract idea; it requires concrete historical social contexts. These contexts were provided by Europe.

The Industrial Revolution

The three most important events of the 200 years of Jewish history from 1800 to 2000 were: the creation of the State of Israel; the creation of North American Jewry and the Holocaust. All three would have been inconceivable without the means of production and transportation provided by the Industrial Revolution.

The first Zionist Congress took place in 1897 in Basle, Switzerland and could not have taken place one hundred years earlier on anywhere near the same scale or format. Around 200 Jews from 17 countries came to Basle at a specified time to discuss the future of the Jewish people. Until the 19th century and the Industrial Revolution such gatherings would have been impossible. In 1797 no railroads and steamships existed and consequently no mass movement of people or large hotels. There were no mass-distributed newspapers (as there were no technical means to produce them or literate market to consume them) and no reliable international mail or telegraph system. The organizational existence of the Zionist movement depended on the Industrial Revolution and so, too, the physical existence of the Zionist enterprise in the Land of Israel.

Early opponents of Zionism frequently used the argument that Zionism was impractical because a wasteland could not absorb millions of Jews. Zionists replied that this may have been true in the past but the technical and engineering skills and the scientific knowledge of the Industrial Revolution would enable them to turn this wasteland into a flourishing garden productive enough to absorb all the Jews who wished to come. This argument was eventually confirmed by the historical record.

Between 1870 and 1914, an estimated thirty million people immigrated to the United States to work in new American industries hungry for labor. This mass immigration was possible because of the new industrial transportation technologies of steamships and railroads. Two million Jews were part of this migration. From a minor Jewish community during the Civil War, American Jewry had become, by World War I, one of the largest and certainly the most powerful and influential community in the Jewish World.

The rise of Nazism and its industrial methods of murder made American Jewry the largest Jewish community in the world by the end of World War II. Democratic Capitalism, the product of the Industrial Revolution, as well as its precondition, made American Jewry the richest, freest, most powerful and self-confident Jewish community in history. American Jewry's power mobilized wisely was one of the preconditions for the creation of the State of Israel, an event that altered

Jewish history and further increased the self-confidence of Jews as American citizens. Industrialization, and the secular Enlightenment values and scientific frame of mind that had made it possible, created new concepts of human civilization and interaction that stimulated German Jewry to create the Reform, Conservative, and neo-Orthodox versions of Judaism — the modern Judaism that by the 20th century had become the new Jewish normal.

The Enlightenment

Even before the Industrial Revolution, the Jews were profoundly affected by other universal developments. Foremost amongst these were the Scientific Revolution and especially its offspring the European Enlightenment. Zionism itself was a late product of the secular humanist Enlightenment. Zionist leaders from Herzl, to Jabotinsky to Weizmann to Ben Gurion propounded Enlightenment values.

There were also inherent parallels between Francis Bacon's maxim that it was humanity's task to *penetrate* Nature and tear her secrets from her and the Zionist imperative to *conquer* the 'wasteland'. Adam Smith and Karl Marx – both products of the Enlightenment – hoped that their endeavors would result in a new man: more rational, just, and moral. This ambition was reflected in the Zionist aim to create a new type of Jew: more independent, less obsequious and more heroic. Without the Enlightenment concept of the *New*

Man, it would have been impossible to develop the Zionist concept of the *New Jew.*

20th century Jewish life was a consequence of the Enlightenment and the development of science and capitalism. Science and commerce were the basis of the modern humanist revolution as well as the prerequisites for eventual Jewish emancipation. Science and commerce are ethnically neutral, and reward competency and imagination regardless of religious or cultural affiliation. Together, they were the basis of a major paradigm shift in human civilization. Countries that took part in this shift prospered, those that rejected it became backward. It was no accident, therefore, that the Netherlands, the foremost commercial polity of its time, possessed a built-in resistance to ethnic discrimination and that Spanish and Portuguese Jews found refuge there from the Inquisition. Renaissance Humanism, the Scientific and Commercial Revolutions it engendered and the European Enlightenment that encapsulated these developments were the prerequisites to Jewish emancipation, the birth of modern Judaism and the modern Jew, and thus the birth of the Zionist project.

The political culture and ideologies of the Zionist Movement and subsequently of Israel were derivatives of 19th century European ideologies: liberalism, socialism, and capitalism, which were products of the Enlightenment and the Industrial Revolution. This had both positive and negative effects.

Positive – because it armed Zionists with practical and ideological tools that enabled them to leverage their inferior numerical strength into superior power in order to withstand zealous Arab opposition to the establishment of the state as well as to create a highly developed economy and one of the best armies in the world. Negative – because it cultivated a certain self-satisfied arrogance regarding their own successes which planted the seeds for its ultimate destruction.

The Enlightenment values of the West and of many of Israel's more secular citizens had evolved in the 21st century; the Enlightenment values of the major political and cultural trends of the Zionist project had deteriorated, thus alienating western support and its own most productive citizens. This alienation weakened the Zionist project from within, which in turn eroded support for the Zionist project from without, which eventually led to the demise of the Zionist project – the State of Israel.

Chapter Three

Modern Nationalism

The Enlightenment gave birth to Modern Nationalism and thus to Democracy – from the Greek *'demos'* (the people) and *'kratos'* (rule); i.e. the people rule. Nationalism and democracy were interconnected because until the Enlightenment, the nation only consisted of the monarchy, the aristocracy, the high clergy, the landowners and the rich merchants. The 'common' people – small farmers, workers, artisans, peddlers, shopkeepers – were not counted. Nationalism changed all that – it depended on the entire nation, including all classes and professions. When Adam Smith wrote *The Wealth of Nations* in 1776 he became one of the first thinkers to characterize the nation as comprising *all* persons of whatever class residing in the state – the aggregate human resources of the nation, the proper management of which can increase the wealth of the nation.

Across the ocean in the same year of 1776, Thomas Jefferson was affirming the identical principle: "We hold these truths to be self-evident, that *all* men are created equal..." The term *all* men [not just the upper classes] is what is operative and revolutionary in the document. The principle that rights pertain to every individual person is based on this sentence and is the keystone to every subsequent civil and human rights struggle: blacks, women, non-citizens, gays etc. The concept of "Rights of the People" evolved in the United States (as it has in the entire Democratic World) to include every man and woman that were citizens of the state ("The Nation") and in the case of the American Constitution to include non-citizens (all *"persons",* not only citizens). Early nationalism was concerned with the social contract between rulers and ruled and the powers and prerogatives of government vis-à-vis the rights of individuals. Hobbes, Locke and Jefferson gave voice to these issues. This might very well be called *Civic Nationalism* or conversely (at least in the case of Locke and Jefferson) *Liberal Nationalism.*

Zionism, as envisaged by Herzl in his futuristic novel *Old-New-Land,* was preeminently liberal in its political and constitutionalist attitudes but was also an *Ethnic Nationalism* in the sense that it strove to advance the inalienable human rights of a particular ethnic group. In this it anticipated the *Liberation Nationalism* of the post WWII anti-colonial milieu and might be considered a proto-*Liberation Nationalism.* In fact, Herzl envisaged an independent Egypt as well as independent self-governing African states long before 19th and 20th century progressives were even hinting at this likelihood. He felt that Zionism must be implemented in concert with the striving for the basic human rights of other peoples (*including* the Arab citizens of the future Jewish state). Marx, on the other hand, was a racist; he had contempt for non-Western cultures (of which, ironically, he included Russia) and even endorsed the idea of imperialism bringing 'civilization' to them, thus setting into motion the industrialization that would bring about the 'inevitable' proletarian revolution that would encompass the entire world.

But Zionism was also a product of 19th century *Romantic Nationalism*, which rejected the political reductionism implicit in the Enlightenment stress on individual rights and embraced a more holistic vision of human well-being that recognized the place of language, culture and homeland in the well adjusted human being – that a human being cannot be a human being *sui generis* but only as part of a greater cultural collective; what Marx would have called 'concrete historical man'. Or as the reactionary monarchist de-Maistre noted: "I have seen, in my time, Frenchmen, Italians, Russians, etc.; I even know, thanks to Montesquieu, that one may be a Persian: but as for *Man*, I declare I never met him in my life; if he exists, it is without my knowledge." Unlike de-Maistre's anti-Enlightenment monarchism, post-Enlightenment *Romantic Nationalism* was essentially democratic, because it derived its legitimacy from the entirety of the nation – the people, language, land, culture and folklore that molded and reflected the nation's personality. In this it was a consequence of the Enlightenment rather than the commonly held view that it was a revolt against it.

The flipside of this development was the subsequent idolatry of the land-working peasant and the negative cultural and political consequences this often engendered. Norwegian author Knut Hamsun's *Growth of the Soil* (for which he received the Nobel Prize in literature in 1920) essentially raised the national peasant experience to a transcendent level bordering on racial mysticism. Hamsun was an ardent Norwegian nationalist and part of the romantic Norwegian nationalist culture that evolved after the Norwegians had liberated themselves from 400 years of Danish occupation and began to create their own national mythology and narrative. He believed that writers should depict the "whisper of blood and the pleading of bone marrow". His subsequent support for Nazism was not some perversion but rather a reflection of a worldview and attitude towards life reflected in his writing. He had previously written that: "The Negros are and will remain Negros, a nascent human form from the tropics, rudimentary organs on the body of white society. Instead of founding an intellectual elite, America has established a mulatto stud farm."[7] Hitler could not have said it more forthrightly. As critic Stephen Holden wrote of Hamsun: "the themes of his nature-loving writing... partook of the same nostalgia for a purified, agrarian utopia as one side of the German fascist vision."[8] In a more diluted form, land worship eventually became an integral part of a certain Israeli mindset; ultimately with catastrophic consequences for the Zionist project itself and ultimately for the Jewish people.

In the 19th and 20th centuries, worship of the past had become the new idol worship of many rightwing political leaders and intellectuals. Nostalgia was the virus that eventually produced the disease of Fascism. In the late 20th and early 21st century it also became a trademark of New Age environmentalism and certain segments of the anti-growth left. As historian Peter Gay noted: "Nostalgia runs deep in the human psyche; it is almost irresistible, all the more so because it generally masquerades as rational criticism of the present (where there is always much to criticize) and rational praise of the past (where there is always much to praise)." He continued: "But nostalgia drives reasonable criticism and ... Praise to unreasonable lengths: it converts healthy dissatisfactions into an atavistic longing for a simpler condition, for a childhood of innocence and happiness remembered in all its crystalline purity precisely because it never existed." He understood that "Nostalgia is the most sophistic, most deceptive form regression can take."[9] Economic historian Eric Roll agreed with Gay and wrote that radical economic and social change generates dissatisfaction that leads people to idealize the past since they "cannot understand the forces which are transforming their own society". He caught much of the current *New Age* radical environmental mindset when he wrote that "The German Romantics of the nineteenth century urged...going back to the...Middle Ages...many of the suggestions for social reform that are finding adherents today have the same romantic quality."[10] This is a mindset to keep in mind when analyzing the psychological attraction of Israel's post 1967 settlement project in the occupied territories.

Unlike anti-Enlightenment monarchism, post-Enlightenment 'liberal' *Romantic Nationalism* was democratically inductive in that authority arose organically and naturally from the nation *in its entirety* and not dictatorially deductive with authority devolving from the top down – from King, or from the Gods or from divine right. But it was unlike *Liberal Nationalism* in that it posited that human freedom was not only a formal/mechanical social contract in which individuals were free to do whatever they wanted, as long as they did not hurt the person and property of another (the central Enlightenment legacy and the very essence of the American political instinct), but was only complete when the ethnic collective that the individual belonged to was free to express its cultural uniqueness, *within and as part of the framework of liberal constitutionalism.*

As the great Italian patriot and political liberal Giuseppe Mazzini (1805-1872) had indicated, individual persons could not be truly free if their people were enslaved or ruled by another people or culturally discriminated against.

There is an inherent wisdom in Mazzini's insight. Individual liberation is meaningless if it requires you to alienate yourself from what makes you uniquely 'you' – what, after all, is that 'you' that you are liberating. Napoleon's demand that in order to achieve rights as individuals, French Jews must give up their collective identity, came to be known in the 20th century as 'cultural imperialism'. It was a demand that invited opposition from both reactionary imperialists and left-wing cosmopolitans.

The individual rights guaranteed in the United States Constitution meant nothing to individual African Americans until Blacks, as a race, were emancipated. The values of the Enlightenment meant nothing to individual Jews until Jews, as an ethnicity, were emancipated. The principles enshrined in the *Declaration of the Rights of Man and of the Citizen* (the fundamental document of the French Revolution) meant nothing to the residents of France's colonies until they gained their freedom from French rule. The *Universal Declaration of Human Rights* could not be *universally* implemented until the *national* liberation of the former colonies took place. (Ironically these former colonies were often ruled by homegrown dictators who violated individual human rights more than the former European imperialists whose rule was often moderated by the *Liberal Nationalist* frameworks they lived by.) In other words *Ethnic Nationalism* very often trumped *Liberal Nationalism* in the decolonization process. Israel was perhaps the only former colony or mandate whose national/ethnic liberation morphed into formal liberal democracy in practice, until it was eventually inundated by the idolatry of land worship which in 2013 and 2014 began to erode the constitutionalist and democratic foundations upon which modern Israel had been built and which had constituted the fundamental worldview of Herzl, Jabotinsky, Weizmann and Ben Gurion.

Romantic Nationalism was inspired by Rousseau and Herder. The latter argued that geography (the land itself) molded the natural economy, customs and social mores of a people; implying that a truncated national geography (land) would not enable the full development of the individual or the flowering of the national culture and thus would not enable a spiritually healthy national population. This romantic nationalist attitude towards the national land infused every ideological shade of Zionism and helps explain many subsequent irrational Israeli policy decisions regarding 'The Land of Israel'. The Romantic Movement tended to mystify nature and therefore *Romantic Nationalism* often stressed the authentic wholeness of those who worked the land as opposed to the atomization and artificiality of industrial society and the supposed dehumanization of those that lived and worked in it.

Romantic Nationalism gave birth to the Tolstoyan view that only peasants were healthy 'authentic' human beings because they worked the land; a view similar to Montaigne's opinion of peasants or Jefferson's view of the yeoman (a free man owning his own farm) as the backbone of society. Tolstoyan ideas about land and authenticity infused socialist Zionist ideology (especially the Kibbutz movement) and were one of the components of the subsequent idolization of the land which morphed into its most extreme expressions following the 6-Day War. *Romantic Nationalism* influenced and was influenced by philosophy, art, music and literature. Hegel's concept of spirit in history, including the spirit of the times (*Zeitgeist*) and the spirit of a people rooted in a particular land (with the state as the concrete expression of that spirit) had great direct and indirect impact on Zionist attitudes towards the Land of Israel and State of Israel. In Zionist thinking, the *Land of Israel* evolved into an icon and the Hegelian concept of the state as the ultimate expression of the spirit of the people became dominant.

Hebrew, unlike English, does not easily differentiate between country and state. In English one can hate one's state while loving one's country – this is almost impossible in Hebrew. *Medinat Ha'Yehudim* is the literal translation of Herzl's *The Jewish State*; the Land of Israel is the literal translation of *Eretz Yisrael*. One could say the land (*Ha'Eretz*); the Land of Israel (*Eretz Yisrael*) or the State of Israel (*Medinat Yisrael*) but one could not say the country of Israel. Because of this, the term *Ha'Aretz* was sometimes used in lieu of country; but it was more often understood as shorthand for the Land of Israel. Thus, patriotism to the country, to the state and to the land became one and the same. Religious Zionism posited that the People of Israel, the Land of Israel and the Torah of Israel were one and the same thing – an indivisible whole (the Jewish equivalent of the Holy Trinity). For them betraying the land was tantamount not only to betraying one's people (i.e. treason) it was also betraying one's God (blasphemy). Betraying the land became betraying the country and the will of God in the eyes of this compact minority. Yitzhak Rabin's political realism subsequently cost him his life as a consequence of this worldview.

Zionism was best described as a form of *Cultural Nationalism*: a nationalism in which the nation is defined by a shared culture. It combined *Ethnic* and *Liberal Nationalism* but, as with elements of *Romantic Nationalism*, focused on a national identity shaped by cultural traditions and by language, not on concepts of common ancestry or race. It thus became an alternative to a religious identity for many Jews. Judaism became the religion of the Jewish ethnic group but an ethnic Jew did not have to be religious. *Jewishness* following the Enlightenment was not dependent on religious observance. And since the various Diaspora Jewish communities had come to reflect different ancestries, religious practices and racial groups, the term *Cultural Nationalism* seemed to be the most suitable for 20th century Jewish identity.

Wilsonian self-determination, a worldview that had historical roots in the 1878 *Treaty of Berlin* which recognized an autonomous Bulgaria and an independent Romania, Serbia and Montenegro, was, in a way, 'Applied *Romantic Nationalism*'. President Wilson's principle of self-determination was an indirect Hegelian acknowledgement that different nations had different 'spirits' and required their own states on their own land to best express it. The recognition of Zionist aims at Versailles was a reflection of this, and despite the common misconception that Zionists based their claim to the Land of Israel on God's promise, Zionists ALWAYS argued their *public* case on the basis of Wilsonian self-determination (even if in *private*, when dealing with Bible-reading Christians they used the religious argument). But *Romantic Nationalism* was a two-sided coin: on the one hand, Mazzini and Herzl with their liberalism and stress on the future, and on the other hand Mussolini and Gush Emunim with their nostalgia for a past that never was. As the Zionist project advanced into the 21st century, these two sides of Jewish *Romantic Nationalism* came into fateful and eventually fatal conflict.

Chapter Four

Historical Zionist Analysis

History matters! Israel was born in 1948 but its gestation in the bosom of the Zionist Idea and Zionist Movement took place almost 100 years preceding its birth. It was this gestation that bred the habits of mind and the political culture of the state after 1948. One cannot understand the political culture that led to the downfall of Israel unless one understands the variations of the Zionist Idea that preceded its birth. One must understand the diverse Zionist attitudes to the Land of Israel, as they evolved out of historic religious attitudes and coalesced with modern European ideologies, in order to understand how these variations converged following the 6-Day War to create an idolatry of the land that trumped all reason, grand strategic self-interest, and existential necessity.

As mentioned, modern Zionism's internal political culture was constituted out of a 19th century amalgamation of

European political culture which included liberalism, socialism, Marxism and social reform, in addition to Hegelian and Kabalistic concepts of the inherent sprit of a people. Yet the *Idea of Zionism* preceded modern Zionism in that it was implicit in the very essence of Jewish tradition. The Jews that actually came to Israel were predominately traditional and observant and saw modern Zionism as a consequence of Jewish tradition, especially as it related to perception of the Land; a perception more reflective of *Romantic Nationalism* than of Enlightenment social contract. This produced an internal struggle within Zionism and often within the individual Zionist regarding the land – between the Enlightenment social contract (utilitarian) view of the land as the means to establish a state, and the land as the vital essence of the national soul as posited by *Romantic* and *Mystic Nationalism.* As Professor Harold Fisch, a national-religious intellectual put it "...the division between the 'Zionists of Zion' and those who supported the Uganda plan of 1903 (*see territorialism below*) was really the fundamental and continuing division within Zionism..." Fisch defined Zionists either as "political schemers who thought in terms of a territorial base for normalizing the Jewish condition..." or as "... those for whom 'Zion' bore its full semantic weight of myth and yearning and for whom the Return carried with it a hope which went far beyond mere national self-determination." He saw the political schemers as advocating a "solution of the Jewish problem ... (as a) means... of ridding the world of the scandal of Jewishness, and the Jewish people of its mystery." He saw the second group as 'Zionists of Zion', who saw Zionism as "the fulfillment of Judaism in acknowledgement of the mystery; it was to be a return to transcendent tasks and origins."[11]

We see, therefore, that the seeds of *Mystic Nationalism* were present at the very outset of the Zionist project but only really flourished after the 1967 war, eventually suffocating other expressions of the *Zionist Idea*. The reason for this was that its emotive power was more accessible to the great masses of Jews that eventually came to Israel because it had deeper roots in the historical Jewish experience. Ben Gurion himself noted that most of the Jews that embraced the modern Zionist idea did not immigrate to Israel and most of the people who did immigrate to Israel after its establishment were not Zionists in the modern sense of the word. But they were Zionists in Fisch's sense; in the religiously organic sense of the word as the vast majority of them were observant Jews who prayed to Zion several times every day and on special occasions and holidays. The majority of European Jews who made Aliyah before the Holocaust – the Polish Jewish 4th Aliyah and the German Jewish 5th Aliyah – were also, for the most part, not self-identified Zionists but simply refugees who had nowhere else to go.

The truth is that 'Zionism' was never one ideology; it was at the outset a *federation* of *common-cause* ideologies, which in the 21st century became a loose *confederation* of *conflicting* ideologies. The only thing that characterized all early Zionists was their propensity for self-criticism. Upon reading the founding ideologues of Zionism, one is impressed that Zionism might have been the most ferocious program of self-criticism in human history. Indeed, many anti-Zionists, noting this relentless self-criticism that excoriated the Jews for their condition rather than blaming the Gentiles, charged the Zionists with simply standing anti-Semitism on its head. But by the second decade of the 21st century Zionism had changed from a common-cause, *self-critical,* meta-ideology into a fragmented ongoing *self-indulgent,* ideological civil war. But let us begin at the beginning.

Political Zionism

Political Zionism was the brainchild of the Viennese journalist and playwright Theodore Herzl (1860-1904). Shocked by rising anti-Semitism in Austria and France he concluded that fighting anti-Semitism was futile and that the only solution to the Jewish problem was political; the creation of a Jewish state. Consequently, he convened a series of 'Zionist Congresses' and established the Zionist Movement dedicated to creating that state. His aim was to obtain a charter from the "civilized" countries of the world granting the Jews sovereignty in a Jewish-owned territory. To this end he met with Kaiser Wilhelm and the Sultan of Turkey, as well as others.

Being an assimilated Jew from the Austro-Hungarian Empire and of a romantic nature, he had been greatly impressed by the rising cultural nationalism of the constituent parts of the Austro-Hungarian Empire (as other early Zionists had been inspired by the Italian *Risorgimento* and by Polish nationalism). In a way, Israel could have been regarded as one of the Austro-Hungarian Empire's successor states. The components of the empire which eventually became independent states or parts of independent states in the 20th century included: Austria, Hungary, Bosnia and Herzegovina, Croatia, the Czech Republic, Slovakia, Slovenia, large parts of Serbia and Romania and smaller parts of Italy, Montenegro, Poland and the Ukraine. It would not be farfetched to include Israel in this list, given the number of Jews from these countries who were involved in Zionist activity and the fact that Herzl's book *The Jewish State* grew out of this political milieu and influenced Jews outside the empire.

Practical Zionism

Practical Zionism preceded *Political Zionism* by several decades. It emphasized concrete, incremental steps to attain Zionist goals despite inadequate political conditions. These included immigration to and rural settlement in Palestine. This policy was adopted by two groups: the 'Lovers of Zion' and *Bilu*, which is a Hebrew acronym for "House of Jacob, let us go [up]" (a verse from the Book of Isaiah). These groups appeared in Eastern Europe in the 1880s and had little overriding political vision. They were more concerned with 'curing' Jews of their ghetto habits and characteristic means of livelihood, mainly by engaging in agriculture in the Land of Israel. The Land of Israel as such was their paramount preoccupation and Tolstoyan ideologies celebrating the land emerged to make this preoccupation coherent. These immigrants were called the *First Aliyah* and they created an embryonic Jewish agricultural community as well as the first Jewish villages (such as *Rishon Le'Zion*) and small workshops.

It was during this period that frameworks for buying land from Arab landlords and absentee Turkish land owners became the prominent element of Zionist activity. The history of land buying, with all its interesting anecdotal stories became a mythological component of Zionist culture in general and Labor Zionist culture in particular. Zionists acquired land; they did not sell it and they certainly did not give it up voluntarily. This was a powerful psychological factor which later on was ignored by international mediators between Israel and the Palestinians. Ignorance of psychological factors on both sides greatly eroded the power of rational arguments in favor of peace.

After Herzl's death, in 1904, hopes of obtaining a political charter in Palestine declined. *Practical Zionism* became the only game in town until WWI and the Balfour Declaration (1917). The champions of this doctrine were many of the Labor Zionists called the *Second Aliyah.* They founded rural settlements on collective and cooperative principles such as the Kibbutz. They built modern towns, and established the first industrial enterprises. But leaders of the *Second Aliyah* (exemplified by Ben Gurion) quickly became identified with an approach called *Synthetic Zionism,* as this best reflected their dedication to the ultimate establishment of a Jewish State and the strategic needs of this aim.

Synthetic Zionism

Synthetic Zionism was a doctrine proposed by Dr. Chaim Weizmann (1874-1952), an internationally renowned chemist, preeminent Diaspora Zionist leader and later the first President of Israel, at the eighth Zionist Congress in 1907. He proposed a synthesis between Political and Practical Zionism: a unified strategy synthesizing the political with the practical. This concept endorsed synchronized action on both tracks: political activity coupled with practical endeavor in Palestine. Weizmann was its most effective advocate. He used the practical achievements of the *First Aliyah* (as well as his own contribution to the British war effort) to obtain the political achievement of the Balfour Declaration, and the political achievement of the Balfour Declaration to advance increased practical activity in the Land of Israel. This included the immigration of distressed Jewry (the Polish immigration of the *Fourth Aliyah* and German immigration of the *Fifth Aliyah*) before WWII; the ultimate political achievement being the establishment of the State of Israel.

Synthetic Zionism's political realism and pragmatic flexibility dominated the Zionist movement from the Tenth Congress (1911) onward and eventually enabled Labor Zionism, under Ben Gurion's pragmatic leadership, to attain hegemony over the entire Zionist project until the *'Ma'apach'* of 1977 when Menachem Begin defeated the remnants of the Labor tradition. Labor's preeminence came about because Jabotinsky and his followers (the precursors to the Likud) remained loyal to a pure Herzliyan *Political Zionism* in the Diaspora while Labor dominated the practical settlement and development work in the Land of Israel; work that excited the masses of Diaspora Jewry and inspired their monetary and political support. Because of this, Labor had natural allies in the Religious Zionist Camp (who perceived actual settlement on the land of Israel as a religious imperative) as well as the various Liberal parties that saw Weizmann as their mentor, as well as with most of Diaspora Jewry. Following the 1967 war, the resurgent 'Land of Israel question' destroyed the 'historical alliance' with the Religious Zionists and splintered Labor Zionism from within.

Spiritual Zionism

Spiritual Zionism was formulated by Ahad Ha'am (1856-1927), also known as the *Secular Rabbi*. He had been one of the leaders of *Hibbat Zion*, the Practical Zionist predecessor to the *Political Zionism* of Herzl. He saw the problem as one of Judaism rather than one of Jewry; that the Jewish people had to reconstruct Judaism in the post-Enlightenment secular age, and that this was the key to Jewish survival. He did not believe that a Jewish state in Palestine could accomplish this and so opposed political Zionism with ferocious vigor – expressing fierce criticism of the Jewish settlers' treatment of the native Arab population. Moreover he argued the physical impossibility of such a small country absorbing all the Jews in the world (unlike Weizmann and Ben Gurion, he did not understand the scientific potential for intensive development). He believed that the renascent Jewish community in Israel (being built by *Hibbat Zion* and others) should act as a 'spiritual' center radiating out a new, mostly secular, Jewish culture to the Jews of the world, regenerating their creative energy and reinventing Jewish culture in accordance with the demands of the Enlightenment and the Industrial Age.

Certain elements of *Spiritual Zionism* were adopted by some of the leaders of *Synthetic Zionism*. For example, Ben Gurion called for the new state to become a 'light unto the nations', mostly because he believed that unless Israel became a 'light unto the nations' it could never become a 'light unto the Jews'. In other words, his view was utilitarian as well as idealistic. Given their unique history, temperament and attitude towards life, the Jews could never become excited by a third-rate mediocre country. Similarly, Weizmann envisioned Israel as a world center of scientific research, solving problems that debilitated all of humankind. As early as 1948, several months before the actual establishment of the state he called for a national project to find an alternative to petroleum – as he had already anticipated the political, economic and security problems petroleum would eventually cause.[12] If this indeed had become Israel's predominant mission, instead of land fetishism, Israel would probably still exist as a thriving and even celebrated nation amongst the other nations of the world. Unfortunately, as Israel did become more and more mediocre (especially in the realms of ethics and morals) world Jewry became more and more alienated from the Jewish state, eventually leaving it to its own devices and to its eventual self-destruction.

Chapter Five

Historical Zionist Politics

Zionist thought combined with Zionist practice to form Zionist politics – the major divisions being Labor Zionism, Revisionist Zionism, Religious Zionism and General (Liberal) Zionism.

Labor Zionism

Labor Zionists felt that Jewish national redemption could not be achieved without social redemption; i.e. without 'curing' the Jews of their ghetto habits which derived from their abnormal social/economic structure. In other words Jewish liberation required a twofold revolution (a double miracle as it were) – the social revolution being both the prerequisite to, and part and parcel of the national revolution. Most laborites were Socialists such as Constructive Socialist Nachman Syrkin (1868- 1924) and Marxist Socialist Dov

Ber Borochov (1881–1917); others were not: for example the Tolstoyan A.D. Gordon (1856–1922), who advocated work on the land as a spiritual therapy; what he called the 'Religion of Work', which for him and his admirers was the only remedy for the 'disease' of the ghetto.

Borochov saw the Jewish social revolution occurring along classic Marxist lines. The Jewish bourgeoisie would build a modern capitalist economy in the Land of Israel, which would create an industrial Jewish proletariat. According to classic Marxist doctrine, this would be an interim economic development which would lay the groundwork for the inevitable internal contradictions of capitalism to develop. This would eventually result in the Jewish proletariat rising up in revolution, taking control of the capitalist means of production and creating a Jewish dictatorship of the proletariat. This was known as 'Revolutionary Socialism'

Syrkin, less intellectual than Borochov but more grounded in reality, thought this was nonsense. He saw how *Practical Zionism* was progressing step by step: one more Kibbutz, one more Moshav, and one more factory…, as well as how almost all 'investments' were actually Diaspora Jewish contributions. He perceived that this was the reality because there was nothing at the time that any self-respecting Capitalist could possibly invest in, so that Borochov (more prominent at the time than Syrkin) was simply wrong. If there was to be a socialist society it must be *constructed* from the ground up and serve as the foundation of the Zionist enterprise; in other words it must be a practical response to the essential conditions of Zionist activity on the ground. This was known as 'Constructive Socialism' which was exactly what happened in practice. Syrkin's genius was recognized after the fact, not as a guideline for action but as a historically correct analysis. In historical hindsight we see that Ben Gurion had been the preeminent Syrkinist, while his more left-wing colleagues remained enamored with the Marxist vocabulary of Borochov and thus were marginalized by the practical reality they themselves were creating with their Kibbutzim, Moshavim and Histadrut enterprises.

By 2014, Labor had become politically schizophrenic – on the one hand just another party framework for political ambition; on the other hand a repository of sincere idealists whose ideology was little more than nostalgia for past glories rather than producing programs suitable for the globalized 21st century. Ironically, Labor's past glories reflected a historical anomaly. Israel was the only country in the democratic world whose historical founding fathers were of the Left. The Left built the country: the economy, the army, the culture, and the social structures. They were the 'establishment' that absorbed the mass immigration; that felt a sense of entitlement (they were Israel's 'Mayflower generation'); they were, therefore, the 'establishment' that earned the resentment of masses of 'newcomers' – mostly from Middle Eastern countries. Menachem Begin skillfully played on this resentment, and in 1977 the Labor establishment was thrown out of office by this other outlier. It was the alliance of the outliers – Begin, the political outlier, and Middle Eastern Jewry, the social/ cultural outlier.

Borochov's primary theoretical contribution had been the concept of the *Inverted Pyramid* which was also quickly invalidated by history. This was a theory of Jewish economic life that described the Jews as an abnormal people; an abnormality that could only be 'cured' by the Jews returning to their ancient homeland and engaging once again in productive physical work. He wrote that 'normal' peoples have a pyramidal social/economic structure: 80% in productive physical work at the base of the pyramid; 15% in services in the middle of the pyramid and free professions; and 5% in intellectual or spiritual work in the peak of the pyramid. With the Jews, however, the pyramid was inverted: 5% were involved in productive physical work (at the base) and 95% in services or intellectual work. The Jews in the Diaspora lived on 'air' (in Yiddish: *Luftmenschen*) not on the productive material work of industry and agriculture.[13] According to Borochov, this socio-economic abnormality is what bred their ghetto habits and thus indirectly contributed to anti-Semitism because it reinforced nationalist stereotypes of the Jews being parasites living off the material work of the authentic nation. Unfortunately, historical fact can really do mischief to some wonderful theories, and Borochov's was no exception.

This is because after WWII, the inherent dynamism of Capitalism revolutionized the occupational structure of the entire developed world, which became an inverted pyramid. By the year 2000 less than 20% of the working population in North America, Europe and Japan were working in industry, agriculture and mining combined. In 1870, 70-80% of the US population had been employed in agriculture; in the 1920s and 30s, 30-40% were employed in manufacturing. By 2012, only 2% of the population was directly employed in agriculture, only 9% in manufacturing and a fraction of a percent in mining. These trends had been universal since WWII. The economy of the world had become 'Judaized'; the occupational *Inverted Pyramid* had become the norm, while classic Labor Zionist ideology still preached that the Jews should strive to correct their 'abnormal' socio-economic pyramid. Such empirical dissonance made Labor Zionism appear pathetic in the eyes of many thinking Israelis; if their arguments were so irrelevant regarding the economy why would they be relevant regarding the occupation and the status of the territories.

Yet, Borochov's other theoretical foundation was solidly reaffirmed by historical experience and reinforced by none other than the self proclaimed bourgeois and founder of Revisionist Zionism, Vladimir Ze'ev Jabotinsky, in his book *The Jewish War Front* (see below). In this theoretical foundation, Borochov had observed that when the Jews were resident in economically undeveloped societies they tended to become the 'middle-class' (traders, artisans, free professionals etc.) of those societies. When the children of the peasants began to strive for a better life in the cities they came into competition with the Jews already occupying these essentially urban occupations and this caused anti-Semitism. This observation was confirmed in Eastern Europe and more recently in the United States, specifically in the 1970s and 80s when the aspiring Black middle class ran into Jewish occupation of commerce and education within the Black ghettos causing a temporary rise in Black anti-Semitism. As Korean store owners replaced Jewish store owners, anti-Jewish sentiment was replaced by anti-Korean sentiment.

Borochov had asserted that Zionism was a historic-economic necessity for the Jewish people and the historic role of spearheading this Jewish national liberation process was reserved for the Jewish proletariat. For him it was the only way to implement the principle of "self-work", which meant living off the work of oneself rather than the work of others and by this creating a new Jew – a 'muscular Jew' curing himself of the ailments of the ghetto with hard physical labor. Self-work for these early labor Zionists also meant self-defense and the 'muscular Jew', redeeming himself not only by work on the land but by military self-sufficiency which meant not being pushed around on one's own land. For socialists of this kind the two were intertwined. This version of socialist Zionism greatly resembled the belief systems of Marxist nationalist hawks like Mao Tse Tung and Ho Chi Min. Indeed one could have drawn many parallels between these socialist Zionists and Maoism – most notably their nationalism, their deep suspicion of the city and the urban intelligentsia and their glorification of agricultural and industrial workers. It was also no accident that the anti-Marxist Ben Gurion was a great admirer of both Lenin and Mao – leaders that combined nationalist patriotism with Socialism.

Borochov's theory of the abnormal socio-economic pyramid became ideologically ubiquitous; it was explicitly or implicitly adopted by every shade of Labor Zionism and even by many Liberal Zionists such as Weizmann and Dr. Arthur Ruppin (1876 –1943), known as 'The Father of Jewish Sociology'. Both were great supporters of the Kibbutz Movement as the most effective instrument of the practical side of *Synthetic Zionism*. In fact it was Ruppin, appointed head of the *Land of Israel Office* of the *World Zionist Organization* in 1908 and charged with directing settlement policy in Palestine, who was instrumental in buying large tracts of land and creating the first Kibbutzim and Moshavim (Degania, Merhavia and Kinneret). He is credited with making *Practical Zionism* possible and paving the way for the unique character of the *Second Aliyah*.

Critics of Zionism often argued that the *Inverted Pyramid* theory was but anti-Semitism stood on its head – that the Labor Zionists had accepted all the stereotypes the anti-Semites had of the Jews and placed the onus of correcting these character flaws on the Jews. There was something to this charge. The essay *Self-Emancipation* by Pinsker implied as much. The Jews had to emancipate themselves from their abnormal exilic existence on two fronts – the objective exilic existence by creating a Jewish State, and the subjective exilic existence by changing their own characteristics and liberating themselves from their own internal ghetto Jewishness. These two emancipations were intertwined: the Jews could not mobilize the energy and force of will to change their objective exilic existence unless they changed their characteristics; but on the way to the state they could use Jewish settlement in the Land of Israel as an instrument to change their characteristics. The land, as such, became transcendently central to the entire labor-Zionist project of self-emancipation; it became the antidote to the disease of exilic Jewry.

Consequently, two major trends of Labor Zionism – followers of the Tolstoyan A.D. Gordon (1856–1922) and the Marxist Yitzhak Tubenkin (1888–1971) – glorified and mystified work on the Land of Israel. Tubenkin was, therefore, not enthusiastic about the establishment of the state in 1948, recognizing that this would limit the ability to liberate the entire Land of Israel. The 1967 War revived the Land of Israel issue and in retrospect must be seen as the beginning of the end of Labor hegemony over the Zionist project. Labor Zionists such as Tubenkin, the leader of a major Kibbutz movement, Nathan Alterman preeminent labor poet, and Rachel Yana'it Ben Ziv, wife of the second president of Israel, labor stalwart and youthful friend of Ben Gurion, were founders of *The Greater Land of Israel Movement* which later allied itself with the Religious Zionists (*Mavdal)* and the Likud and made land worship the center of Israeli political discourse until its self destruction.

Ironically, ultra-right wing *Gush Emunim* became a latter-day manifestation of Marxist Borochovism – promoting the entire Land of Israel to cure the diseased Jewish soul. People who resisted this approach were treated as if they had some sort of ideological Munchausen's disease – people who were in love with their own sickness. The Labor Zionist analysis of the Jewish dilemma was thus recruited into the service of a self-destructive right-wing policy that had fatal consequences.

Revisionist Zionism

Revisionist Zionism was a militant expression of Herzl's *Political Zionism*. It was propounded and led by Vladimir (Ze'ev) Jabotinsky (1880-1940) who, in opposition to Weizmann, advocated a 'revised' (more radical) policy towards the British. The story of Revisionist Zionism is, in many ways, the story of this one man. He molded Revisionist Zionism in ways that no single individual molded Labor Zionism. In 1925 Jabotinsky established the *Revisionist Zionist Alliance*, which advocated unremitting pressure on Great Britain to attain Jewish statehood on both banks of the Jordan River in order to attain a Jewish majority in Palestine.

His views can be summed up as follows: Jews demand equality not because they are an ancient civilization, nor because they have disproportionately contributed to human progress; Jews do not demand equality because they are more virtuous than others; Jews demand equality of rights *only* because they are *also* human beings.

Jabotinsky, therefore, was opposed to Labor Zionism's conditioning national salvation on class struggle and the creation of a Jewish working class. He advocated *Had Ness* – 'one miracle' – the national miracle, completely independent of any perceived social miracle, as the most direct way to create national independence. Nevertheless, once the state was created, Jabotinsky agreed that it could be a laboratory for the entire human race. In *The Jewish State – Solution to the Jewish Problem* published in 1936 he wrote:

> Many among us believe that the Palestine of the future will become a laboratory where the cure for the redemption of the whole of mankind will be discovered and achieved in our own special way. However, before we set out to discover the remedy we must first build the laboratory...[14]

Previously he had endorsed the notion of the Jewish state being *a light unto the nations*:

> ...a Jewish state is not an end in itself. It is but the first phase in the process for the attainment of 'Greater Zionism'. This will be followed by the second stage – the return of

the Jewish people to Zion, the end to the Diaspora and the solution to the Jewish problem. The real and final aim of 'Greater Zionism' will appear only in the third phase, for which, in fact, all great nations strive – the creation of a national culture which will serve as a shining example to the world as is written: 'For out of Zion shall go forth the Law'.[15]

He also criticized Labor's idolization of the working class. He did not think that the bourgeoisie were an inferior species within the social ecology. Indeed, he felt they were the drivers of progress more than the proletariat and often proudly declared that he was bourgeois. Moreover, he anticipated certain technological developments with the same kind of futurist clarity as Weizmann and Ben Gurion. In 1940, several months before he died, he projected that technological progress would advance so rapidly that in the not too distant future, technology would replace all drudge work, all physical labor, all production and that the proletariat as a class would disappear and only the bourgeois intelligentsia would remain. Thus he concluded the long term prospects of the underlying social analysis of Labor Zionism were infinitesimal. Yet his own observations led him to conclusions very similar to Borochov's regarding the causes of certain kinds of anti-Semitism. In his book *The Jewish War Front* he differentiated between German anti-Semitism (the anti-Semitism of men – a hatred of the

Jew as a Jew) and Polish anti-Semitism (the anti-Semitism of things – a hatred of the Jew based on economic antagonism [Borochov's thesis]).

This nuanced approach to types of anti-Semitism highlights Jabotinsky as one of the most complex and multifaceted personalities produced by the Zionist Movement. He was a novelist, poet, essayist, political philosopher, linguist, ideologue, party leader and soldier. He was fluent in six languages – Russian, Italian, French, German, Hebrew and Yiddish – and could carry on a reasonable conversation in about 20 more. He translated Israel's national poet Bialik into Russian. He translated Edgar Allen Poe's *The Raven* into Russian and Hebrew. He also translated the *Rubayyat* of Omar *Khayyam* and one-third of Dante's *Inferno* into Hebrew. He advocated writing Hebrew in Latin characters and to this end learned Maltese (a Semitic language written in Latin letters) in order to develop a system. He wrote two novels.

Jabotinsky developed the notion of *Hadar* (literally majesty), reflecting his keystone ideological axiom that "every man is a king"; i.e. inherently majestic in his own personhood. *Hadar* advocated that Jews must always behave with courtesy, civility, concern, consideration for others, punctuality, punctiliousness, neatness and cleanliness.[16] Yet with all this he probably was one of the most maligned leaders in the history of the Zionist project. This caused resentment amongst his devotees (like Begin and Shamir) and explained a great deal of Israeli political behavior after the *Ma'apach* of 1977[17] - behavior that more often than not remained a mystery to Israel's friends in the West.

Jabotinsky had great foresight in many areas and was totally blind in others. A dedicated liberal constitutionalist in political principle and personal temperament, his infatuation with all things Italian led him to sympathize and even support Mussolini before the alliance with Hitler. Some Jabotinsky acolytes, such as Abba Achimeir and many in *Lehi* (the Stern Gang) proudly declared themselves to be unrepentant fascists even after WWII, while Begin's *Herut* followed more in the liberal footsteps of Jabotinsky, at least until 1967.[18] This division had historical consequences. The descendents of Jabotinsky's Revisionist party were first the Herut Party and subsequently the Likud Party. In these parties both trends lived side by side. The classic Revisionists, though certainly on the far right of the political spectrum, were classic constitutional democrats, while others in Herut were populists deeply suspicious of constitutionalism and inclined to the kind of majoritarian democracy that can easily degenerate into fascism.

The Likud primaries of 2012 prior to the 2013 elections drove out the last remaining Revisionists - Benny Begin (Menachem Begin's son), Michael Eitan and Dan Meridor - for, amongst other reasons, defending the Supreme Court's constitutional decisions that reversed policies and actions supported by the settlers. Bibi Netanyahu became the most leftwing MK on the Likud list. Yet he purged Reuven Rivlin, a classic Jabotinsky Revisionist, from his role as Speaker of the Knesset for defending, in the Begin tradition, the constitutionalist principles of the Knesset against anti-constitutionalist proposals of the Likud. Ironically, in 2014, Rivlin became the 10ᵗʰ President of Israel despite Netanyahu's vigorous opposition and largely because 5 leftist Labor MKs voted for him, out of respect for his constitutionalist behavior while Speaker of the Knesset.

Jabotinsky was an interesting combination of cynicism and idealism as well as nationalism and constitutionalism. This characterized many of his political offspring. He was convinced that there was no peaceful way for the Jews to regain any part of Palestine. He believed that the Arabs were a proud people and would fight. He had contempt for left-wing attitudes that if the Jews were nice the Arabs would accept them. He thought this attitude was condescending towards the Arabs. He believed that if the Jews wanted a homeland they would have to crush the Arabs militarily. But he also believed that Arab citizens should have complete equality in a Jewish state. In 1934 he drafted a constitution for the future Jewish state which stated that Arabs would be equal to Jews "throughout all sectors of the country's public life." The communities would have equal duties and equal rights and "in every cabinet where the prime minister is a Jew, the vice-premiership shall be offered to an Arab *and vice versa*

(Italics mine)."[19] He also demanded complete equality for the Arabic language in the Hebrew-speaking Jewish state. On the other hand, Jabotinsky was almost pathologically suspicious of the good will of others. Previously (July 18, 1910), in an essay entitled "Man Is a Wolf to Man", appearing in the Russian periodical *Odesskie Novsoti* he wrote:

> Stupid is the person who believes in his neighbor, good and loving as the neighbor may be; stupid is the person who relies on justice. Justice exists only for those whose fists and stubbornness makes it possible for them to realize it.... Do not believe anyone, be always on guard, and carry your stick always with you— this is the only way of surviving in this wolfish battle of all against all.[20]

Yet in the very same essay he expressed an extraordinary empathy with the plight of Black people in the United States. He voiced moral outrage at white pogroms in which 20 Black people were killed, following the July 4th, 1910 victory of Jack Johnson over Jim Jeffries for the heavyweight championship of the world. He wrote:

> Since it was the black man that won and there was a suspicion that other blacks in the land would feel proud, the white citizens of the great republic could not tolerate this...They sought to quash black pride and fell upon blacks in a proportion of 50-to-1, smashed heads, trampled people and acted cruelly even to women and children... In the United States, the freest republic on earth, there are ten million citizens suffering a shocking lack of rights simply

because of the color of their skin... in America, there is plain and simple hate of one race against another—a devious hate, right before our eyes, arbitrary, without reason and without cause.[21]

Every Likud prime minister, from Menachem Begin to Benjamin Netanyahu, was a protégé of Jabotinsky's views. Western leaders advocating for Israeli/Palestinian peace at the time could not comprehend this mental environment and thus could not understand Israeli policy under the Likud or the resentment Likudniks harbored for Labor Zionists because of their treatment of Jabotinsky (branding him a fascist). Most importantly, they could not understand how many Likudniks could sincerely believe they could pursue the Greater Land of Israel policy and still be fair to the Arabs. Not understanding this mental inner life, the initiatives of western interlocutors always failed, with catastrophic consequences for both Jews and Palestinians.

Religious Zionism

Religious Zionism represented a fusion of Jewish religion with nationhood. It advocated that Jewish political freedom had become a prerequisite for the vitality and relevance of the Jewish religion. But it also felt that Judaism as a religion was an unconditional necessity for a vigorous Jewish national life in the homeland. In 1902, the Fifth Zionist Congress decided to consider cultural activity as part of the Zionist program. In consequence, Rabbis Yitzchak Reines and Ze'ev Yavetz established the *Mizrahi* organization. In this political context *Mizrahi* is the Hebrew acronym of *merkaz ruhani* or "spiritual center" which they wanted Israel to be (*Mafdal* became the political party in Israel that represented this worldview). The spiritual center concept was analogous to Ben Gurion's 'light unto the nations' view of Israel, and until the Six Day and Yom Kippur Wars (and subsequent creation of Gush Emunim) was one of the reasons *Mafdal* was the natural ally of Labor Zionism. But while Ben Gurion's followers were rational messianists (recognizing the limitations of power) the founders of *Gush Emunim* had become mystical messianists. *Mystical Nationalism* began to impose itself more and more on the language of political discourse in Israel.

Mizrahi held its first world convention in 1904; its platform, concerned itself with observance of the commandments and return to 'Zion'. In Palestine, Rabbi Avraham Yitzhak HaCohen Kook gave religious Zionism his endorsement as he regarded settlement in the Land of Israel as the prerequisite for ultimate redemption. This morphed into the sincere belief (difficult for others to comprehend) that compromise on the land issue would not only endanger Jewish redemption *but also the redemption of all humanity*. For them the biblical prophecies were literal. The Jewish People were 'chosen' by God to redeem all of humankind, but they could not do this outside of their own homeland or only in part of their homeland. Any suffering inflicted on the Palestinians was rationalized by the sincere religious Zionist as follows: 'you are suffering for a short period of time in order that we Jews can redeem the world.'

In Palestine, religious Zionists devoted much of their efforts and resources to constructing a national-religious education system. *Hapoel Hamizrahi* (literally "The Workers Spiritual Center") broke from *Mizrahi* to focus on Orthodox rural settlement in Palestine under the slogan *"Torah va-'Avoda"* (Torah and Work). The general spiritual atmosphere of this movement was very close to A.D. Gordon's "Religion of Work". In 1956, *Mizrahi* and *Hapoel Hamizrahi* united as the National Religious Party (*Mafdal*), the political descendents of which were still very active in Israeli politics in 2014, and which formed the bulk of the settler movement. For religious Zionists, fidelity to the land was a divine directive and even talk about dividing the land with another people was sacrilegious.

Here again semantics played a part in Israeli political discourse. What had been meant by the term "The Jewish State"? Was it a state for the Jews (for Jewry as an ethnicity) as proposed by Herzl, Weizmann, Ben Gurion and Jabotinsky, or was it Jewish in the sense that it was to be organized according to Jewish religious practice? The second definition would have been favored by almost half of the Jewish population (National Religious, ultra-Orthodox, and many traditional Middle Eastern Jews). This created emotional, psychological and religious constraints that deeply affected Israeli politics.

These roadblocks to serious compromise with the Palestinians were never really appreciated by American and European interlocutors, or respected by the Israeli Left. Resentment against what was perceived as condescending contempt for deeply held beliefs exacerbated emotion-laden political discourse which, in turn, hampered rational policy making.

Of course there was a limit to the extent a non-religious person could respect these particular deeply held religious beliefs. For while playing the constitutionalist and democratic game, religious Zionists rarely denied that their eventual vision was to create a state run by Jewish Law *(Halacha)*,[22] much like the Islamists advocating a state run by *Sharia* Law. *Mafdal* (National Religious Party) was the political party that represented this worldview, which had a firm footing in Rabbinic Zionist literature.[23]

Mafdal's founders had been Middle European Jews who, while devout, were greatly influenced by the moderating influence of European Liberalism and Socialism. Following the Six Day War, some of the more prominent members of this party even advocated the internationalization of the Old City of Jerusalem, including all its religious sites (even the Western Wall). But the children and grandchildren of the founding generation, being born in Israel, were influenced more by Middle Eastern attitudes towards the *actuality* of the land (rather than the *idea* of the land). This caused them to become increasingly less liberal. They were the demographic that established *Gush Emunim* and the proactive settler ethos. Eventually their ideological offspring became the completely radicalized and intolerant 'hilltop youth' who saw it as a *mitzvah* (a religious virtue) to harass the Arab residents of the occupied territories. Being theocrats, they saw the constitutionalist institutions of the State as their enemy. In the 2013 elections some 20 MKs sympathetic to this ideological temperament were elected to the Knesset. The 'spiritual' imperative of religious Zionists and its negative impact on Israeli policy and subsequent Jewish survival cannot be underestimated.

General (Liberal) Zionism

General Zionists might be referred to loosely as "free market constitutionalists". Initially the term referred to non-party members of the Zionist Organization, but they eventually created their own institutions and the *Organization of General Zionists*, was established in 1922 as a centrist party in the *World Zionist Organization*. They favored private initiative and protection of middle-class rights. The more conservative among them might be compared to America's Republican Party while the more socially minded to America's Democratic Party. The first group eventually evolved into Israel's Liberal Party, the second group eventually evolved into Israel's Independent Liberal party.

The Liberals ultimately joined with Herut to form Gahal (the precursor to the Likud) in an attempt to end Labor hegemony.

The Independent Liberals felt more comfortable with Labor and were often in Labor-led coalition governments. Both wings, however, were pragmatic and non-ideological in relation to the land question. Sadly, this pragmatism did not stand them in good stead following the 6-Day War as territorial compromise and settlements gradually became the central issue in Israeli political discourse. This was a discourse that did not favor nuanced argument – you were either for or against and the Liberals were rather like Tevye in Fiddler on the Roof – "on the one hand..." but "on the other hand..." The Liberals were eventually subsumed into the Likud and disappeared as a distinct ideological stream moderating the right. The Independent Liberals suffered more or less the same fate vis-à-vis Labor. Following the 6-Day War ideological definitions of Right and Left gradually came to mean one's position on security and foreign policy affairs (the Land of Israel issue primarily) and less on economic and social issues.

One reason was that globalization joined with the fall of the Soviet Union and the capitalist revolution in China to turn all Social Democratic parties in the West into modified free marketers. Mitterrand's privatization efforts in France, New Labor in Britain, and the unvarying economic pragmatism of the German Social Democratic Party, all converged to completely change the tone of moderate left political discourse all over the Western World. Moving towards the center, Social Democrats began to occupy and thus constrict the political space of European Liberals. This affected Israel's political discourse as well, especially in the 90's when Israel's high tech revolution was set in motion. Israel became the *Start up Nation* and the globalized high-tech entrepreneur became the new icon of the Zionist project – replacing the sweaty *Halutz* (agricultural pioneer) as the hero of Israeli society. Venture capital and spectacular 'exits' quickly replaced the image of the rugged *Halutz* braving Arab hostility in the service of the Zionist project. No one celebrated and boasted about the *Start up Nation* more than Labor icon Shimon Peres.

Yet the disease of nostalgia still prevailed (much like the conquest of the West in highly urbanized America) and the task of satisfying the national mythology of the *Halutz* fell to *Gush Emunim* – they were the last *Halutzim*, the last remnant of the authentic 'New Jew', the aim and essence of the Zionist project. As one commentator of the time noted "...the reason some on the left had sympathy for the Gush Emunim settlement movement in the West Bank is tied to the sense that the settlement movement breathed life into an ethos that had faded away."[24] Rational political discourse had difficulty competing with this cognitive dissonance regarding the national narrative and this had negative impacts on Israel's political decisions, for which the ideologically castrated Israel Liberals had no answer.

Labor's historic devotion to practical settlement became subsumed by kibbutz guru Yitzhak Tubenkin's more absolutist view of settlement. As mentioned above Labor personalities such as Tubenkin, Natan Alterman, and Rachel Yana'it Ben Zvi created *The Greater Land of Israel Movement*. This quickly attracted the young leadership of the nationalist religious Kibbutz Movement – a movement which combined the practical settlement ethos of the Labor Movement with their mystical attachment to the land of the Bible. Needless to say, this paved the way for the ascendance of Begin in 1977. Revisionist attitudes towards the Land of Israel had been affirmed and facilitated by the main factors of Labor Zionism and land fetishism became the dominant theme of Israeli political discourse –ultimately causing great injury to the Zionist project.

Chapter Six

The Land of Israel
in Jewish Thinking

"Whenever a people loves the soil of its native land more than its own life, it is in danger – as all the peoples of the world are – that, though nine times out of ten this love will save the native soil from the foe, and along with it, the life of the people, in the end the soil will persist as that which was loved more strongly, and the people will leave their lifeblood upon it."[25]

Franz Rosenzweig

Land fetishism was not some kind of outlier in a greater more liberal Jewish historical tradition as many on the Zionist left proposed. There is no question that social justice was a major factor in the Jewish tradition (the prophetic tradition that the Zionist and Jewish left hung their hats on) but it was in no way so dominant that it submerged the centrality of the land in forming the historical Jewish persona. This chapter presents an overview of the ancient and medieval religious and cultural underpinnings to the centrality of the Land of Israel in the Jewish mind and its consequent impact on Israeli policy making. This is most exemplified by S.D. Goitein's description of the transformation of Middle Eastern Jewish society from an agricultural society to a commercial society under Muslim rule."As many transactions could legally be made only in 'connection with soil' they adopted the legal fiction that every Jew ideally had a part of the soil of the Holy Land". Goitein goes on to describe how "Hundreds of documents have been found in the *Geniza* (Cairo archives) in which one party confers upon another four square cubits of its share in the Holy Land 'together' with this or that right, *which forms the real content of the contract* (italics mine)." Contracts were "listed as 'transfer of land', but (this was only a) legal fiction."[26]

Ben Halpern, in *The Idea of the Jewish State*, subsequently wrote that the "... Jews remained always conscious of an irreducible alienhood ... in all lands but the ancestral home." Because of this "However ancient and intimate their bonds with any other land, their destiny and true home, they knew, were elsewhere." Consequently, "the Land of Israel remained the ultimate as well as the original homeland of the Jews."[27]

One can only understand how the idolatry of land warped Zionist policy by keeping Goitein's and Halpern's words in mind, and realizing that the Jewish population of Israel in 2014 was 30-40% orthodox religious in one form or another and that another 30-40% (mostly of Middle Eastern Jewish background) considered themselves traditional, and only a minority were truly secular in the Enlightenment tradition. The irony is that all the architects of Zionism were products of the Enlightenment who used Enlightenment political and cultural thinking to construct Israel; but the vast numbers of people who came to Israel had little or no Enlightenment pathos. Their 'Zionism' had much deeper cultural and religious roots than Herzl's and the other 19th century thinkers that formulated the various versions of Zionism.

These were people whose very conception of themselves as Jews, whose very self-consciousness of themselves as Jews, was tied to the powerful symbols, biblical events and personalities of and within the Land of Israel. These were the people most susceptible to the simplistic slogans of Gush Emunim; especially as these slogans were like lyrics sung over the background music of Arab and Muslim contempt for Jewish history and for the Jews per se; a contempt that not only denied that the Jews had any historical *right* to the Land of Israel but that the Jews did not even have any historical *attachment* to the Land of Israel. These were the Israelis (especially Middle Eastern Jews) who resented Western politicians and left-wing Israeli intellectuals lecturing them that these Arab and Muslim attitudes were of no consequence and that if Israel only gave up the conquered territories and established a Palestinian State these attitudes would vanish and Israel would be accepted in the Middle East.

Middle Eastern Jews, like the Arabs, had come from an honor society and took such disdain much more seriously than European Jews did; they were as unforgiving to insult as the Arabs. Given the personal experiences of their parents and grandparents (many of whom had fled to Israel from the Arab world with only the clothes on their backs; their property confiscated by ultra-nationalist Arab governments) they also felt that Arab and Muslim attitudes towards the Jews was not conditional on Jewish political behavior but rather was inherent in their culture, and really had nothing to do with the settlements or the territories. Moreover, the mystic tradition of the *Kabala* had persisted in Middle Eastern Jewry and to some extent in European Jewry (mostly Hassidic Jews). Kabalistic mysticism (unlike other mystical traditions) favored the collective over the individual mystic experience. As Gershom Scholem put it "... the spiritual experience of the mystics was almost inextricably intertwined with the historical experience of the Jewish people ... rarely did the Kabbalist speak of his own way to God ..."[28]

Many of the settlers and their supporters were imbued with this Hassidic/Kabalistic spirit. Appeals to a policy of territorial withdrawal based on the rights of the Palestinians fell on deaf ears. The only time appeals to a policy of territorial withdrawal worked effectively in Israeli political discourse were when they were based on self-interest. But like left-wing intellectuals everywhere, the Israeli iteration could not resist the temptation to demonstrate its own moral superiority by writing and speaking nastily against the "racism" and cruelty of Israeli society. This explains why, after the Second Intifada, the Zionist Left all but disappeared in Israel; they were like a stomach upset which the Israeli body politic vomited out.

One anecdote will serve to demonstrate how left-wing love of their own moral superiority and condescension towards people not of their sort hurt their own cause. After the Rabin assassination a settler Rabbi horrified by the consequences of settler education did a public *mea culpa* which caused him to be boycotted by his fellow settlers. He had publically contemplated the possibility that eventually the Jews might have to give up large parts of their sacred homeland for the sake of the greater virtue of peace. In response to this potential terrible trauma he proposed that the day of the evacuation become a day of mourning; that Jews sit *shiva* (the traditional seven days of mourning), rending their clothes and fasting. He suggested that the occasion become part of the *Tisha B'Av* narrative – the day the Jews fast and mourn the destruction of the Temple and the expulsion from Spain.

Almost immediately leftists wrote articles condemning this attitude which proved that the Rabbi was really a fascist because he did not recognize the real reason for getting out of the territories, which was to set Israel right with the

Palestinians. Any settlers who might have identified with the Rabbi's views were immediately deterred from joining the Rabbi in the attempt to reform Gush Emunim. This was the Israeli version of Bobby Kennedy's observation that liberals were never happier than when they were going down to defeat together in a good cause. This was a case of the Left preferring to be cleverly derisive rather than politically effective.

Zion and Zionism

Zionism derived from the word Zion, which designated both the Land of Israel as a whole and Jerusalem specifically. Its emotive significance became manifest after the destruction of the First Temple and the subsequent Babylonian exile. Psalm 137 includes these words:

> "By the rivers of Babylon, /there we sat down, yea, we wept, /when we remembered *Zion*... Sing us *one* of the songs of *Zion*. How shall we sing the LORD's song in a strange land? If I forget thee, O Jerusalem (*Zion*), let my right hand wither. If I do not remember thee, let my tongue cleave to the roof of my mouth; if I prefer not Jerusalem (*Zion*) above my chief joy."

During the wedding ceremony the groom recites "If I forget thee, O Jerusalem (*Zion*), let my right hand wither". Observant Jews prayed to Jerusalem (*Zion*) three times a day, saying:"Blessed are You, God, the builder of Jerusalem...May our eyes behold your return to *Zion* in compassion. Blessed are you God, who restores His presence to *Zion*." After every meal observant Jews prayed:

> Have mercy Lord, our God...on Jerusalem Your city, on *Zion* the resting place of Your glory, on the monarchy of King David Your anointed, and on the great and holy Temple upon which Your name is called...Rebuild Jerusalem, the holy city, soon in our days

At the conclusion of *Yom Kippur* and *Passover* Jews said "Next Year in Jerusalem (*Zion*)" and when consoling a mourner, Jews said "May God comfort you among all the mourners of *Zion* and Jerusalem." Three of the most prominent Jewish holidays were *Passover*, *Shavuot* and *Succoth*; pilgrimage holidays that required the entire Jewish populace living in the Land of Israel and proximate Diaspora to make a pilgrimage to the Temple in Jerusalem. After the destruction of the Second Temple, the actual pilgrimage was no longer obligatory, but was celebrated virtually in prayer and ceremony.

There were also agricultural holidays with special prayers and customs appropriate to the environment and climate of Israel, but yet mandatory upon Diaspora Jews living in a completely different climate to celebrate. For example it was compulsory on *Succoth* to pray for rain because the six-month 'dry season' of the Land of Israel was about to end and the six-month 'rainy season' was scheduled to begin and Jews wanted to hasten it with prayer. Observant Jews in Canada would say this prayer on *Succoth* even though it had been raining all summer and was snowing at the time of the prayer. The centrality of the Land of Israel was paramount in religious observance since the Romans expelled the Jews from their land and tried to erase their memory by renaming it Palaestina (after the Philistines).

Settlements and the Inertia of Historical Pathos

It is instructive to remember the chronology and the historical pathos of the settlement project as it relates to Israeli attitudes immediately after the 6- Day war. The pre-State *Gush Etzion* settlements (Kfar Etzion, Massu'ot Yitzhak, Ein Tzurim and Revadim) are a good case in point. The settlements were built on land legally purchased in the 1920s, and during the War of Independence were a frontline of defense of Jewish Jerusalem. Ben Gurion said "If there is a Jewish Jerusalem today, the Jewish people owe their gratitude to the defenders of *Gush Etzion*". These settlements were completely surrounded and besieged by the Arab Legion and local Arab irregulars for over six months, and on May 13, 1948 when Kfar Etzion finally surrendered, 127 of its inhabitants were slaughtered by the Legion and Arab irregulars. The inhabitants of the other villages were taken prisoner and their homes plundered and burned.

The saga of Gush Etzion and the role it had played in Israel's collective memory, was analogous to the siege of the Alamo (which fell after only 13 days) in the collective memory of the United States. Yet, even so, the reconstruction of Gush

Etzion was initially resisted by Israeli leaders despite massive public pressure. That is until September 1, 1967 when the Arab League met in Khartoum and issued the infamous *Three No's of Khartoum*: No recognition of Israel. No negotiations with Israel. No peace with Israel. Given the Arab contempt this declaration revealed, the demand to reconstruct Gush Etzion became politically inexorable and began several weeks later. Human beings are driven by symbols, and the reconstruction of Gush Etzion must be seen as a symbolic statement of the Jews in Israel that they were not to be taken lightly and treated with contempt. Thus resentment, more than ideological, political or security concerns, was the motivation for a project that over the next 50 years morphed into the greatest mistake of the Zionist enterprise – the settlement project.

The very fact that any peace process had to be conducted within rationalist and utilitarian parameters; that claims to the land had to be treated equally by interlocutors and thus had to ignore (or even acknowledge) the special relationship of the Jews, eroded the enthusiasm of many Jews for the peace process itself at a very deep psychological level. Especially, as the Palestinians (and other Arabs) insisted on rubbing the Jews' noses in it by denying that the Jews even had a unique historical and cultural attachment to the land. The chronic resentment this caused amongst large portions of the Jewish population spilled over into political discourse and policy making and caused the Jews to make political decisions based on resentment and indignation, which in retrospect, can now be seen clearly as catastrophic.

Chapter Seven

The Failure
of Jewish Territorialism

Territorialism was a Jewish phenomenon that had been evolving for over a half a century before any kind of Zionist thinking. It advocated for a sufficiently large Jewish territory that would enable Jews to live in safety not dependent on the good will of others. Nothing highlights the centrality of the Land of Israel for Jewish identity than the failure of Jewish territorialism. Even Theodore Herzl, the founder of modern political Zionism, did not comprehend this centrality. Being a semi-assimilated Jew Herzl did not necessarily believe that the Land of Israel had to be the new Jewish Homeland. In his 1896 book *The Jewish State* he proposed Argentina as a possible alternative. Herzl did not have that organic attachment to the Land of Israel that Jews with deep cultural roots did.[29] Land, for him, was utilitarian with no inherent cultural value. At the 6th Zionist Congress, following the 1903 Kishinev Pogrom, he supported accepting the British Government's proposal to settle Jews in Uganda[30] as a temporary solution for Jewish distress (a 'Night Shelter' as he called it). But the representatives of Russian and Polish Jewry- the Jews he was trying most to help and who were the most persecuted in the world – walked out in protest at the very thought of this blasphemous proposal.

In 1825, Mordechai Noah, an American Jewish playwright, attempted to establish a Jewish refuge on Grand Island in the Niagara River, with Christian Zionist encouragement. It was to be called *Ararat*, after the resting place of Noah's Ark. He purchased land on the island and inscribed a cornerstone which read "Ararat, a City of Refuge for the Jews, founded by Mordecai M. Noah in the Month of Tishri, 5586 (September, 1825) and in the Fiftieth Year of American Independence." This initiative was met with Jewish indifference and the project began and ended with the ceremonial laying of that cornerstone.

In 1891, three years before the Dreyfus Affair and six years before the First Zionist Congress, the German Jewish philanthropist Baron Maurice de Hirsch (1831-1896) created the *Jewish Colonization Association (JCA)*. The goal of the JCA was to encourage mass Jewish emigration from Russia and Eastern Europe in order to settle them in agricultural colonies on lands purchased by the Association. Hirsch had been inspired by the establishment in 1889 of the agricultural colony of *Moisésville* named in his honor (his full name being Maurice *Moses* Hirsch) by a group of Russian Jews in Santa Fé, Argentina. The tribulations of these settlers motivated him to establish the JCA in order to help them, as well as establish other Jewish settlements in Argentina. The JCA reached the peak of its activity in Argentina in 1930, with over 20,000 Jews (including the famous Jewish *Gauchos*) on approximately 1,500,000 acres of land. But town life eventually trumped the romance of the soil, and by 1966 only 8,000 Jews remained in these settlements. By the year 2012, only a few dozen elderly Jews were left.

The JCA attempted something similar in Brazil in 1904 with Jews from Bessarabia (modern day Moldova). This colony failed and was liquidated in 1928. Another colony was founded in 1909 but was abandoned even before WWI. The JCA resettled it, but this experiment finally ended in 1965. Another failed attempt was in the 1930s with German Jewish refugees. The JCA was active in the United States and Canada, and in cooperation with other groups had established 78 Jewish farms by WWI in New York, New Jersey, Pennsylvania and Connecticut – the most famous being Woodbine, New Jersey. By WWII JCA activity in the United States had all but ceased. In Canada, 40 Jewish farms had been established by 1930 – the first being the 'Hirsch' colony in Saskatchewan in 1892 (building on earlier Jewish territorial initiatives). By 2012, nothing remained of these attempts.

In 1897 the JCA established three small colonies of Russian Jews in Cyprus at the request of the British Government. This venture failed. In 1891, the JCA bought land near Smyrna Turkey to establish an agricultural training center, called *Or Yehudah* (Light of Judah). The center was closed in 1926. A small Russian immigration to Turkey led the JCA to establish an immigration bureau in Constantinople Istanbul) in 1910. They bought land in Anatolia and Thrace, and founded three agricultural settlements for several hundred Russian Jewish families. But as former residents of Turkey's enemy in World War I they were forced to leave. By 1928 these settlements had been liquidated, and the immigration bureau reinvented itself to assist Jews in transit to Palestine.

In 1934 Soviet authorities, encouraged by Stalin and Jewish Communists established the autonomous Jewish region in *Birobidzhan* in far eastern Siberia on the Chinese border. It was meant to be an alternative to Zionism for the Jewish working class. The Jewish population peaked in 1948 at around 30,000. In the 1959 census the Jewish population had declined to 14,269. In 2002, there were only 2,327 Jews and by 2010 there were only 1,628 Jews left; another colossal failure of Jewish territorialism.

The Uganda Controversy and its Consequences

When the Uganda scheme was rejected by the Zionist Movement, the immediate response was the establishment of the Jewish Territorial Organization (JTO) by British Jewish playwright Israel Zangwill and British Jewish journalist Lucien Wolf. Zangwill, a friend of H.G. Wells, was the first to use the phrase "the melting pot" in his play of the same name describing the American immigrant experience. Wolf was a prominent journalist active in fighting for Jewish rights. Zangwill had been a Zionist; Wolf had not, but like Baron Hirsch advocated the establishment of Jewish colonies in the Diaspora. Zangwill blamed the premature death of Herzl in 1905 on the merciless criticism by East European Zionists of Herzl's advocacy of the Uganda scheme. He wrote:

> Herzl is dead: he worked for his people as no man ever worked for them since Judas Maccabaeus. His people called him dreamer and demagogue, and towards the end men of his own party called him traitor and broke his heart. He worked for his people: they paid him his wages and he has gone home.

In 1905, the 7th Zionist Congress formally and finally rejected the Uganda Scheme and Zangwill and Wolf established the JTO dedicated to "obtaining a large tract of territory (preferably within the British Empire) wherein to found a Jewish Home of Refuge". Zangwill became its president. The JTO attempted to acquire territory suitable for Jewish settlement in Galveston Texas, Alaska, Angola, Australia and various places in Asia. It did not succeed. The JTO declined rapidly after the 1917 Balfour Declaration and was dissolved in 1925.

Uganda was *still* a term of derision in Israeli political discourse
well into the 21st century – over 100 years after it had been
put to rest. The settler movement often called Israeli peace
activists willing to give up the West Bank as "Latter-Day
Ugandists". Even worse the 'peaceniks' were sometimes called
Philistines because the Israeli State, in their vision, would
be limited to the coastal plain – the biblical homeland of
Philistia – rather than the true ancestral home of the ancient
Hebrews, the mountains of the biblical Judea and Samaria.
The settlers positioned themselves as the "Zionists of Zion", to
use Professor Fisch's evocative phrase, while Israeli peaceniks
were not genuine Jews because they had no intrinsic feeling
for the full weight of historical and religious myth inherent
in the words "The Land of Israel".

This put Zionist advocates for territorial compromise in
the grotesque position of having to protest that their love
for the land was no less than that of the settlers and that it
would pain them to have to give it up. These protestations
did not have the same emotive force with the Israeli public
as the "pure" line of the settlers, especially as the Zionist
peaceniks were advocating the same practical steps as the
post and anti-Zionist advocates. Guilt by association is
difficult to overcome. So that even in 2014, when over two
thirds of Israel's Jewish population polled were supportive
of territorial compromise, the peace camp was seen as less
authentic than the settlers by many Israelis, and thus in
many ways less trustworthy. This was reflected in one of

the paradoxes of Israeli elections – a more or less moderate and pragmatic electorate electing increasingly nationalist and uncompromising governments.

Israeli "Territorialism"

Ironically, the most successful territorialist activities were in the Land of Israel; initiatives that had a positive impact on Jewish Life in Israel until 2048. As early as 1896, the JCA began providing financial support for the Jewish settlements of Gedera, Ḥadera, Nes Ẕiona, and Mishmar HaYarden. In 1899, Baron Edmond de Rothschild transferred the settlements he had founded to JCA's management and donated 15,000,000 francs for their further development. In these settlements the JCA introduced modern cultivation techniques and continued to purchase land in the Galilee. It founded other settlements such as Yavne'el, Beit Gan, Kfar Tavor, and Sejarah (Ben Gurion's first home in Palestine). It was involved with the plans to drain the Hula swamp, reconstruct Be'er Tuvia and establish the settlements of Kfar Warburg, Nir Banim, Sdeh Moshe, Kfar Maimon, and Lachish. By 1955, Israel had become the primary field of activity for the JCA. In cooperation with the Jewish Agency (the executive arm of the World Zionist Organization), it helped develop the Upper Galilee. It also provided aid to 30 immigrant settlements. It established credit facilities for agriculture and provided financial aid to Israeli educational institutions well into the 21st century. These included Mikva Israel, ORT, and the agricultural faculty of the Hebrew University in Rehovot.

It is instructive that the ONLY settlements and projects established or managed by territorialists that survived and prospered had been in the Land of Israel. The centrality of the Land of Israel was thus demonstrated empirically. No Western leader, no matter how friendly or supportive of Israel, ever really understood the emotive power of the entire Land of Israel for Jews and how calls for territorial compromise or slogans like 'land for peace' grated on the Jewish nervous system much like chalk on a blackboard. This non-intentional insensitivity to the mood of the Jewish electorate created a constant and ongoing psychological stumbling block to real negotiations and became one of the Israeli right's greatest electoral assets – the implication being that 'the goyim were treating us in a condescending manner'. All other territorialism, other than Zionism, was utilitarian – to give the Jews a safe and productive haven. Only in Zionism did the land have an inherent historical, cultural and theological significance with the great mass of the Jewish people and this was its trump card in regards to any other territorial solution to the Jewish Problem. The evocative nature of the very word Zionism and its identification with the deepest recesses of the Jewish soul, Jewish tradition and Jewish history, as well as its identity with every corner of the Land of Israel as described in the Bible was a major subtext to the modern Zionist narrative and a major driver of significant elements within the modern Zionist movement. For some elements of Orthodoxy, a Jew could not truly be a Jew, could not truly be holy, except in the Land of Israel.

Thus the *subtext* of tradition became the *prime text* of the Zionist story and Enlightenment Zionism was eventually submerged by it, to the disastrous detriment of the Zionist project and the Jewish people.

Chapter Eight

The Land of Israel in Christian Thinking

From the Crusades onward, the Holy Land had been central to Christian thinking and Christian Europe's power politics. For example, the immediate causes of the Crimean War were disputes over Christian sites in the Holy Land between various Christian European countries. The Muslim Ottoman Empire was in decline ('the sick man of Europe') and being pressured by Russia regarding the rights of the Orthodox Church in Israel. The French and British viewed this as a Russian ploy to gain territory and power in the Middle East and they allied with the Ottomans to defeat the Russians. Eventually all Christian churches in Israel (including the Orthodox) were granted official equality by the Ottomans as a consequence of the war, and this was the basis for subsequent power politics in the Middle East.

This event was actually a subheading of a phenomenon called Christian Zionism. Various strains of Christian Zionism provided non-Jewish tailwind to late 20th century and early 21st century Zionist land fetishism. Following the Reformation, many Protestants in the English speaking world, especially the Puritans, began advocating for the return of the Jews to their historical homeland, which they saw happening in conjunction with the Jews accepting Christ as their Messiah and thus hastening the Second Coming. These included such English Puritan notables as John Owen (1616-1683) and Samuel Rutherford (1600–1661) as well as notable colonial Puritans such as Increase Mather (1639-1723) and John Cotton (1585–1652). Ezra Stiles, a prominent Congregationalist theologian and president of Yale College from 1778 to 1795, also supported the restoration of the Jews to their ancient homeland. In 1818 President John Adams expressed the wish for an independent Jewish country in the Holy Land, and that there they would become Unitarian Christians. In 1844, a distant ancestor of Presidents Bush (also named George Bush) – a professor of Hebrew at New York University – called for restoring the Jews to their ancient land where hopefully they would become Christians and hasten the Second Coming of Christ.

British Christian Zionism

Ideas favoring the return of the Jews to their ancient homeland became prominent in England during the 1830s. These ideas were often a conjoining of genuine biblical faith and

British imperialist interests. British evangelist John Nelson Darby (1800-1882) was the originator of *Dispensationalism*, which posits that Israel is distinct from the Church, and that God will fulfill his promise to the Jews by returning them to their promised land. "A land without a people for a people without a land", in its various forms, was a coinage of British Christian Zionists, not of the Jewish founders of modern Zionism. As early as 1843 Christian Zionist Rev. Alexander Keith wrote that the Jews are "a people without a country; even as their own land...is in a great measure a country without a people". A reviewer of Keith's book expressed the same sentiment more concisely as *a land without a people and a people without a land.*

Anthony Ashley Cooper, 7th Earl of Shaftesbury, was a prominent reformist British politician. He fought for reforms in treating the insane, improving conditions in factories and mines, as well as in education and others. For both religious and political reasons he also fought for the Jews and advocated settling Jews en masse in Palestine. In 1853 he, too, wrote that Southern Syria (Palestine) "was a country without a nation in need of a nation without a country". Previously, in 1838, he had lobbied for a British consulate to be established in Jerusalem. In 1839, the Church of Scotland sent a mission to report on the condition of the Jews in Palestine. By 1840, the British government was already considering Jewish restoration. William Hechler (1845-1931) was an English clergyman of German descent and Chaplain of the British

Embassy in Vienna where he befriended Herzl and supported Herzl's diplomatic activities. A publication about Herzl noted that Hechler was: "not only the first, but the most constant and the most indefatigable of Herzl's followers".

American Christian Zionism

The Theodore Herzl of American Christian Zionism was William Blackstone (1841–1935), an American evangelist who, appalled at the persecution of Russian Jews, wrote the *Blackstone Memorial* in1891; a petition in favor of giving Palestine back to the Jews. He wrote:

> What shall be done for the Russian Jews? It is both unwise and useless to undertake to dictate to Russia concerning her internal affairs...Where shall 2,000,000 of such poor people go? Europe is crowded and has no room for more peasant population. Shall they come to America? This will be a tremendous expense, and require years...Why not give Palestine back to them again? According to God's distribution of nations it is their home, an inalienable possession from which they were expelled by force...Why shall not the powers which under the *Treaty of Berlin* in 1878 gave Bulgaria to the Bulgarians and Serbia to the Serbians now give Palestine back to the Jews? These provinces, as well as Rumania, Montenegro and Greece were wrested from the Turks and given to their natural owners. Does not Palestine as rightfully belong to the Jews? ... for they never abandoned the land. They made no treaty; they

did not even surrender. They simply succumbed, after the most desperate conflict, to the overwhelming power of the Romans.

The petition was signed by 413 prominent Christian leaders including future President of the United States William McKinley, Chief Justice of the U.S. Supreme Court Melville Weston Fuller, John D. Rockefeller, J.P. Morgan, Cyrus McCormick, as well as senators, congressmen, newspaper editors, and religious leaders of all denominations before being presented to President Benjamin Harrison. The petition anticipated many of the ideas that Theodor Herzl propounded five years later in *The Jewish State* (1896). When learning of Herzl's Zionist project for the Jewish people, Blackstone became an outspoken and passionate supporter of Zionism. He later chastised Herzl for even considering an interim Jewish state in Uganda and actively campaigned against it. He reportedly sent Herzl a Bible highlighting explicit biblical references to Jewish restoration exclusively to the Land of Israel. The inertia of this Christian Zionist devotion to the land of Israel on behalf of the Jews was to continue well into the 21st century.

Supreme Court Justice Louis Brandeis learned about the Blackstone Memorial in 1916 when he was head of the American Zionist movement. He asked Nathan Straus, founder of Macy's and ardent supporter of the Jews in Palestine, to write to Blackstone, on his behalf. Strauss wrote:

Mr. Brandeis is perfectly infatuated with the work that you have done along the lines of Zionism. It would have done your heart good to have heard him assert what a valuable contribution to the cause your document is. In fact he agrees with me that you are the Father of Zionism, as your work antedates Herzl.

Brandeis understood that grassroots American Christian support for the Zionist cause was vital and asked Blackstone to reissue his *Memorial* for presentation to President Wilson. Blackstone's activities in this regard are considered by many historians to have helped President Woodrow Wilson publically endorse American Zionism and the British Balfour Declaration. Blackstone levered the fact that President Wilson was a religiously observant Presbyterian to secure the endorsement of his *Memorial* from the Presbyterian Church. An historical irony, given that by the beginning of the 21st century the various factions of the Presbyterian Church had begun to support boycotts of Israel.

Joseph Smith, the founder of Mormonism, felt that "the time for Jews to return to the land of Israel is now." In 1842, he sent Orson Hyde, an original member of the founding *Quorum of the Twelve Apostles* of the Mormon Church to Jerusalem where he composed a prayer which contained these words: "(I) consecrate this land unto Thee, for the gathering together of Judah's scattered remnants, according to the predictions of the Holy Prophets – for the building up of Jerusalem again after it has been trodden down by the Gentiles so long, and for rearing a Temple in honor of Thy name." In 1979 the Jerusalem Foundation established the *Orson Hyde Memorial Garden* in Jerusalem in his honor.

Christian Settlement in the Land of Israel

The residual attraction to the Land of Israel is perhaps best exemplified by the history of Christian settlement in the land of Israel even by Christians who were not Zionists. Christian initiatives to settle in Israel in 19th century were as numerous as Jewish initiatives. This attraction evolved in the late 20th century into unrestrained evangelical support for the most right-wing Israeli attitudes towards settlement in the Land of Israel; a support that the Jewish right-wing unreservedly welcomed even though it was motivated by the Christian co-option of the special Israelite covenant with God; a co-option that had deep roots in Church dogma.[31]

The Templers are perhaps the most prominent example of modern Christian settlement in the land of Israel. They were a breakaway sect of German Lutheranism and considered themselves as God's chosen people (Jews having failed in this mission). In this they were not unlike the Pilgrim and Puritan settlers of colonial America (see below). German Christian Zionism first appeared in the 18th century, but the 19th century Templer movement coincided nicely with the power politics of 19th century European powers. Their goal was to rebuild the Temple of Solomon – thus the name

Templers (not to be confused with the medieval *Knights of the Templars*). They were to establish seven communities in Israel.

A small group settled in Haifa in 1868 – fourteen years *before* the first modern Jewish wave of immigration – and established what is now known as the German Colony of Haifa. Its main street eventually became Ben Gurion Blvd. and extended from the foot of the Baha'i Temple terraces to the sea and became a fashionable avenue of cafes and restaurants. *Sarona*, later to become the location of the headquarters of the Israel Defense Forces in the center of Tel Aviv, was established in 1871, 38 years before the Jews had even established Tel Aviv in 1909. The German Colony (*Ha'Moshava Ha'Germanit*) in Jerusalem eventually became an upscale Jewish neighborhood. Overflow from the Haifa Templers established a settlement in *Bethlehem of the Galilee* in 1906, while a splinter group of Evangelical German Protestants established a settlement called *Waldheim* in 1907. *Wilhelma* (named after King Wilhelm), near Ben Gurion airport (once called *Wilhelma* airport) was established by Templers in 1902. *Wilhelma* became a Jewish village after the establishment of the state.

The Templers introduced small industry and many modern 'innovations', such as regular transportation services between Jaffa, Akko and Nazareth as well as the initial stages of a postal service. In the first years of the Zionist settlement in

Israel the Templers helped the Jewish pioneers a great deal. But events in Germany gradually led them away from their religious messianic roots into the political messianism of Nazi Germany and by 1937 34% of the Templers were card-carrying members of the Nazi party and swastika flags were seen in Tel Aviv, Haifa and Jerusalem. The Templers were eventually expelled by the British. Some Hebrew and Yiddish speaking Templers enlisted in the German army and were used by the Nazis to interrogate Jews.

Other Christian settlements included the American-German Colony (*HaMoshava HaAmerika'it-Germanit*) next to the Neve Tzedek neighborhood in south Tel Aviv. It was originally called *Adams City* after the Protestant *Restorationist*[32] from Maine who established it. It was soon joined by German Protestants related to the Templers. The American Colony Hotel in Jerusalem was founded by Protestant Americans and Swedes. After 1948, several Christian communities were established in Israel – in the Galilee and in Zichron Yaacov. The Mormons built a branch of their university in Jerusalem – ironically on land donated by Israel Sieff, the British Jew who personally drove Weizmann to his fateful meeting with Balfour and who initially financed the establishment of the Daniel Sieff Institute which evolved into the Weizmann Institute of Science.

It would have been difficult to maintain that Jews should have been less attached to the entire Land of Israel than

Christians, and since Evangelical Christians had become a major factor in the 21st century Republican Party, they conditioned their support for candidates on their attitude towards Israel in general and for settler Israel in particular. They became a much larger force for the settler mentality than American Jewry; to the ultimate detriment of Israel and of American Jewry.

Chapter Nine

Jews and "Others"

Modern Jewish history was not as unique as many Jews and non-Jews seemed to think. The same forces that affected the Jews in the 19th and 20th centuries affected many other peoples and the history of these peoples sometimes affected the Jews. This chapter will look at just a few. The purpose is to put the Zionist project into a more general context and thus gain greater understanding of its inspirations and its subsequent failures.

Italian Nationalism

Nineteenth century Italian history influenced not only Zionist leaders and thinkers, but many others struggling for national liberation in the name of universal ideas, such as Gandhi, Nehru and Sun Yat-Sen. Mazzini especially, had tremendous impact on 20th century democratic and internationalist thought, including Woodrow Wilson's views on self-determination. Parallels between Zionism and the Italian *Risorgimento* are numerous. Both were self-conscious, purposeful evolutions of national identity into modernity inspired by the 18ᵗʰ century European Enlightenment and the 19ᵗʰ century industrial revolution; reinventing their national cultural heritages within historical continuity. Both were preoccupied with the ethical and cultural aspects of their activities as they related to the political thought of the Enlightenment. The Italian *Risorgimento* anticipated many of the same ideas and arguments of the early Zionist thinkers and had tremendous impact on some of the major players in the Zionist project – from the socialist Moses Hess to the anti-Socialist Ze'ev Jabotinsky.

Moses Hess (1812-1875), a proto-Zionist, applied *Risorgimento* ideas to the Jewish people. He had been a colleague of Marx and had 'converted' Engels to communism; but after the failure of the revolutions of 1848 he began to envisage liberal democracy as reflected in *Cultural Nationalism* as the vehicle for revolutionary change – that every nation had its own inherent spirit that could contribute to the general welfare of humanity. Greatly influenced by the Italian *Risorgimento*, especially the thinking of Mazzini (who was the first to envision a European Federated Super State composed of progressive nation-states), Hess wrote: *The Revival of Israel: Rome and Jerusalem, the Last Nationalist Question* (1862) in which he described how the reconstitution of Israel would contribute to the general welfare of all humanity. He believed that "humanity comes in nationalities ... that humanity is vindicated through the mediation of nations and nationalities ... When I work for the rebirth of my own people, I have not given up my humanistic efforts."[33] Similarly, Mazzini believed that "being a member of a nation one is also a member of the human race and that the only way to belong to humanity is to belong to a specific nation".[34]

Following Mazzini's intellectual lead, Hess conceived of "Judaism as religious humanistic nationalism with an historical mission"[35] and offered compelling arguments for the Jews to redeem themselves by redeeming the Land of Israel and thus enable themselves to contribute to all humanity. This attitude of mind impressed itself directly and indirectly on the future course of all trends of Labor Zionism in particular. At the other end of the ideological spectrum Jabotinsky was greatly influenced by the Italian *Risorgimento*. His hero was Garibaldi. In his autobiography Jabotinsky wrote:

> If I have a spiritual homeland, it is Italy, much more than Russia.... All my views on nationalism, the state, and society were developed during those years under Italian influence; it was there that I learned to love the art of the architect, the sculptor, and the painter, as well as the Latin song.... At the University (of Rome) my teachers were Antonio Labriola and Enrico Ferri, and the belief in the justice of the socialist system, which they implanted in my heart I

kept as self-evident until it became utterly destroyed by the Red experience in Russia. The legend of Garibaldi, the writings of Mazzini, the poetry of Leopardi and Giusti have enriched and deepened my superficial Zionism; from an instinctive feeling they made it into a doctrine.

His moniker at the University of Rome, which he attended for two years, was *Vladimiro Giabotinsky*. His social essays included a complete philosophy of the welfare state, based on a combination of Mazzini's social worldview and the social philosophy of the Bible.

Unfortunately, 19th century *Romantic Nationalism* easily degenerated into 20th century *National Mysticism*. Just as Mazzini's *Cultural Nationalism* deteriorated into Mussolini's *Mystic Nationalism* in the middle of the 20th century, so Ben Gurion's *Cultural Nationalism* deteriorated into the settlers' *Mystic Nationalism* in the 21st century. *Mystic Nationalism* saw the nation as a divine entity. It was related to *Romantic Nationalism* but went beyond healthy attachments to one's national language, food and culture and descended into a "mystical veneration of the nation as a transcendent truth".[36] However, Italy's descent into Fascism did not call into doubt the right of the very existence of the Italian state; in contrast, the rights of the very existence of the Jewish state were called into question for much more minor transgressions. Such double standards contributed to the general resentment of the Israeli electorate, making them immune to even justifiable criticism. The consequences for the Zionist project were disastrous.

Polishism and Judaism

Many early Zionists were Jews from Poland and Belarus who were greatly influenced by Polish Nationalism, which had constituent parts similar to Zionism and which developed in ways analogous to Zionism. Ben Gurion, Begin and Shamir all attended the University of Warsaw during the most intense period of Polish Nationalism. Jabotinsky was a great admirer of Polish Nationalism. Given the tremendous overlap between Polish Catholicism and Polish Nationalism in Polish identity, one might justifiably consider Polishism as a semi-*synecdoche**, analogous in some ways to Hinduism and Judaism (see below).

The intellectual and cultural climate of the early 19th century engendered Polish ambitions for self-government and liberation from foreign dominance. Polish intellectuals were influenced by the Romantic Movement's stress on culture and language[37] as the basis of ethnic identification. As with Zionism, *Cultural Nationalism* quickly led to *Political Nationalism*. The national poet Adam Mickiewicz (akin to

---

* The literal meaning of this word is "simultaneous understanding". It is a figure of speech in which a term for a part of something is used to refer to the whole of something, or vice-versa: for example Hollywood for the movie industry or Washington for the Federal Government or City Hall for the Municipal Government, or conversely the Internet for the World-wide Web or America for the United States.

Israel's national poet Hayim Nahman Bialik) concentrated on patriotic themes and the glorious national past. Chopin's music was infused with the tragic history of Poland. As with Zionism it was the intelligentsia (and in the case of Poland some of the aristocracy) that initiated nationalist sentiments, with the peasant masses slowly being won over. As with Western Europe and the United States in the 18th century the concept of nationhood came to include all persons in Polish society, replacing the old class-based "noble patriotism" exemplified by the *Sarmatism* movement which characterized the Polish nobility from the 15th to the 18th centuries, and which in the 19th and 20th centuries typified a particular exaggerated courtliness amongst Poles of all classes; especially towards women. Some Polish Jews were greatly influenced by this behavior – foremost amongst them was Menachem Begin, the consummate 'Polish' gentleman.

Like Pinsker, many 19th and 20th century Polish nationalists insisted on self-emancipation. They linked self-emancipation to social justice and political modernization which included emancipation of the serfs and adoption of republicanism; in other words, the emancipation of Polish society and culture from its pre-Enlightenment characteristics by way of the hard social, economic and cultural work of the Poles themselves.

At one point Polish Nationalism took a turn that resembled the *Practical Zionism* of the First Aliyah. It was called "Organic Work" (*Praca organiczna*), which aimed to strengthen Polish society at the grass roots through education, economic development, and modernization. Its advocates saw it as a strategy to combat repression while awaiting an eventual political opportunity to achieve self-government.

General Jozef Pilsudski, the dominant nationalist figure between the two world wars, led the fight for Polish independence. He opposed anti-Semitism and was supported by many Polish Jews. Pilsudski influenced Jabotinsky almost as much as Garibaldi and Mazzini. "Jabotinsky even suggested in a 1935 speech before Beitar [Betar] members in Krakow that soil from Trumpeldor's grave in Palestine be brought to Josef Pilsudski's grave as a symbol of the two national movements' close relations."[38] Pilsudski's military thinking was emulated by Jabotinsky followers. As Professor Eran Kaplan noted, "... young Revisionists saw in Pilsudski a leader who actually used his army to achieve concrete, recognizable goals... the founders of the Irgun were inspired by the example of Pilsudski's military organization in Poland."[39]

Pilsudski and other Polish Romantic Nationalists saw the Poles as a "chosen people"; 'chosen' to act as the shield of western civilization, with a mission to civilize the Eastern Slavs, (much as some early Zionists saw their mission to civilize the Arabs and later the Middle Eastern Jews). Like early Labor Zionists, Pilsudski felt that socialist ideology should be merged with nationalist ideology, since that combination offered the greatest chance of restoring Polish independence.

Like Zionism, Polish *Romantic Nationalism* morphed into messianism. Polish messianism saw its mission as the salvation of mankind. It became a mystification of the Polish nation. As with de Maistre and Mazzini, Polish messianists felt that nations determine the fate of humanity. They felt that the Polish nation had been assigned the role of messiah to all the nations of the world. Mickiewicz actually considered the Polish nation to be the "messiah". Poles were the chosen amongst nations and Poland was the "Christ of nations".

Similar to the national religious wing of the Zionist movement, they sincerely felt that Polish national liberation was a prerequisite for universal salvation. Mickiewicz wrote:

> For the Polish Nation did not die. Its body lieth in the grave; but its spirit has descended into the abyss, that is, into the private lives of people who suffer slavery in their own country.... For on the Third Day, the Soul shall return to the Body; and the Nation shall arise *and free all the peoples of Europe from Slavery* (italics mine).

Polish independence in particular preoccupied Woodrow Wilson's concept of self-determination. The 13th of Wilson's *Fourteen Points* was explicitly dedicated to Poland; it might have been termed the 'Balfour Declaration' of Polish self-determination:

> An independent Polish state should be erected which
> should include the territories inhabited *by indisputably*
> *Polish populations* (italics mine), which should be assured
> a free and secure access to the sea, and whose political
> and economic independence and territorial integrity
> should be guaranteed by international covenant. (*A more*
> *"Zionist" statement cannot be imagined – substitute Jewish*
> *for Polish and you have the very essence of Zionism*)

The following anecdote published by the Jewish Telegraphic
Agency in 1926 is a concrete example of the ambivalences
and ambiguities of Polish and Jewish relations in the 20th
century, highlighted at the end by the metaphor of the Exodus
as representing Polish national aspirations.

> The extent of Jewish participation in the struggle for the
> independence of Poland, in the early days of the movement,
> unrecognized by the Great Powers and Polish public
> opinion at large, was impressed upon the public mind
> yesterday when Josef Pilsudski, first Marshal of Poland
> and leader of the Legionnaires, kissed publicly a Jewish
> invalid who fought in the Legion.

> A highly dramatic scene was enacted when the twelfth
> anniversary of the crossing by Pilsudski's Legion of
> the frontier of Congress Poland was celebrated at the
> Legionnaire Congress, opened yesterday in Kielce, the
> first Polish city to be occupied by the Polish Legion under
> Pilsudski's command in 1914. Many Jewish Legionnaires
> were present at the celebration. Pilsudski publicly kissed a
> Jewish Legionnaire who lost both his legs on the battlefield.

M. Stpiczynski, editor of "Glos Prawdy," Pilsudski's organ, in his address, stated that Poland, like the Jews in the desert, must wait another forty years for a new, free generation to arise.[40]

Similar to Zionist messianism, some Polish Messianists were rationalists and others mystics. Edward Abramowski, one of the founders of the Polish Socialist Party was, like Tubenkin, a state-rejecting socialist who advocated for the cooperative organization of society and, like A.D. Gordon, was influenced by Leo Tolstoy. Other views evolved that can only be described as Polish Fascism, displaying contempt for the rights and lives of other peoples (best exemplified by modern Polish anti-Semitism); not unlike the most militant factions of the settler movement who actively cultivated a disregard for the dignity of other peoples. But certainly unlike them in that the active cooperation of hundreds of Polish villages in the slaughter of Polish Jewry during the Holocaust never called into question the very right of the Polish nation to have a Polish state. Delegitimization was reserved for the Jewish state only; thus anti-Zionism morphed into a postmodern iteration of anti-Semitism.

Pan-Turkism

Pan-Turkism (analogous to Pan-Slavism, Pan-Germanism and Pan-Iranism) had no impact on the Jewish national movement, but was in many ways it's contemporary, and is but another demonstration that Zionism was not unique. It had its roots in *Jadidism*, a Central Asian Islamic progressive reform movement which, at its inception, encouraged critical thinking over unquestioning obedience to religious law. It promoted modern education, equality for women, and tolerance for other faiths as well as openness to European culture. In other words its foundations were progressive in every sense of the word. It was an Enlightenment movement that advocated for the modernization of Muslim life much like Zionism advocated for the modernization of Jewish life. But, in response to the expansionist Russian Imperialism of the 1880s it morphed into a national liberation movement for all Turkic Peoples and increasingly came to resemble *Ethnic Nationalism* with growing national mystical tendencies that were eventually held partially responsible for the Armenian genocide – an outrage that never resulted in questioning the very right of the Turks to have their own Turkish state.

Hinduism and Judaism

In many ways, the development of Hindu identity was a mirror image of the development of Jewish identity. Hinduism, like Judaism, related to the religious tradition of the Hindu peoplehood. The technical linguistic term describing this twofold/overlapping connotation is *synecdoche* (see definition above). Judaism as the religion of Jewish peoplehood is an element of Jewish Civilization; while various Hindu groups representing an assortment of ethnic/cultural/spiritual expressions are elements of a greater spiritual civilization called Hinduism.

Hindu is a word first used in the 14th century by Persians and Arabs, not by the Indians themselves. Up until the 18th and 19th centuries it referred to the peoples that inhabited the Indus valley, not to a particular faith tradition. 'Hinduism', understood as a religious or faith tradition, became common in the 19th century under British rule. Many modern researchers (Western *and* Indian) have claimed that Hinduism as a religion in the western sense of the word was invented by British Colonialism in the 1800s. Categorizing the numerous folk traditions and spiritual expressions of the Hindu peoples under one religious classification in order to contrast it with Islam and other religions made it easier to rule India more efficiently. Dealing with one overriding category rather than 1,000 different sub-categories simply made things less complicated administratively. This is not to say that the word 'Hinduism' does not convey a rich and intricate spiritual attitude towards life that *is* unique to the people called Hindus; only to say that it cannot be related to only as a religion – just as the term Judaism cannot be related to only as a religion. In fact, traditional Hindu hostility to Islam *before* the English was not religious; it stemmed from the Hindus' perception that the Muslims were *foreign* barbarian invaders. In other words it was more a 'national' objection than a 'religious' one.

Hinduism after the English invasion became the 'religion' of the Hindu people just as Judaism after the Enlightenment became the 'religion' of the Jewish people. The variety of ethnic groups, cultural traditions and variations of religious or non-religious observance amongst the Hindus was just as diverse (if not more so) than amongst the Jews – yet no one could deny that Hindu identity was as authentic and unifying as Jewish identity. Hindu Nationalism calling for autonomous sovereignty and statehood for this diverse peoplehood can be seen as analogous to Zionism.

The mixture of Hindu Nationalism and spiritual uniqueness that characterized the reaction to English rule was at the outset humanist, cosmopolitan, international, and liberal – i.e. in the spirit of the European Enlightenment. Pioneers of this mixture included Ram Mohan Roy, Swami Dayananda, and the renowned Sri Aurobindo. Like the early Socialist Zionists, they all called for a radical reconstruction of Hindu society. They opposed the caste system and called for equality for women as well as openness to the world. They wanted to reconstruct Hindu life totally. Aurobindo's views were reminiscent of Mazzini's and similar to early progressive Zionism. In the essay "Idea of India" the historian Peter Heehs quoted him:

> Political freedom is the life-breath of a nation; to attempt social reform, educational reform, industrial expansion, the moral improvement of the race without aiming first and foremost at political freedom, is the very height of ignorance and futility... The primary requisite for national progress, national reform, is the free habit of free and

healthy national thought and action which is impossible in a state of servitude.[41]

Heehs observed, in *Religious Nationalism and Beyond*, that Aurobindo's: "models of political transformation were the French and American revolutions and the Italian *Risorgimento* ... his political writings echo Jefferson's and Rousseau's: India based its claim to freedom on 'the inalienable right of the nation to independence'".[42]

These political philosophies were accompanied by what one might term a Hindu *Spiritual Nationalism*; a feeling that Hindu spiritualism had a special contribution to make to all of humanity. These views were similar to Rabbi Abraham Isaac Kook – the dominant figure in the rise of religious Zionism and the first Ashkenazi Chief Rabbi of British Mandatory Palestine. Aurobindo felt that Hindus were 'chosen' "instruments of God to save the light, to save the spirit of India from lasting obscuration and abasement"[43]. Rabbi Kook also felt that the Jews had a special spiritual spark in their souls and his arguments were also redolent with metaphors of light. Modern Hindu nationalism strove to unite Hindu society by breaking down the boundaries of caste, language and ethnic group; just as Zionism wished to unite Jewish society by breaking down the boundaries of class, language and ethnic group.

Gandhi's views about the inviolability of the entire land mass of India and his violent objections to the partition of India would have done credit to the most fervent supporter of the *Greater Land of Israel Movement*. He was reported to have said: "Vivisect me, before you vivisect India". Some researchers have concluded that Gandhi's view of India as a Hindu Holy Land alienated many Muslims and was a major contributing factor to the eventual bloodbath of the partition and it's millions of refugees. How the radiant humanism of Sri Aurobindo and the spirituality of Gandhi declined into the depravity of the Indian civil war paralleled how the love of the land of the Tolstoyan Zionist A.D. Gordon declined into the depravity of the settler movement. The difference being that India's tribulations did not call into question the very legitimacy of the Hindu state. This was a difference that infuriated the Israelis almost to madness and drove them to irrationality in policy making. Even the Nazi era did not call into question the legitimacy of the existence of the German state.

Israel's political culture was derived from the same factors that were influencing the entire globe – factors that were western in origin. Pan-Turkism was influenced and inspired by developments in the West, as was Indian Nationalism. Japanese Nationalism in the 19th century was not only a reaction to the West; it was composed of philosophical and political components of the West. Its economic policies were taken from Alexander Hamilton and its educational system from Prussia. China became Communist; Hong Kong, Singapore and South Korea became Capitalist. Their political and economic systems were not Confucian, they were Western. Every African country eventually developed institutions and judicial systems that derived from the West, not from their own traditions. Only Israel was attacked as being an artificial state because it built itself on western models instead of Middle Eastern models. This double standard infuriated Israelis to the extreme and the subsequent resentment contributed greatly to its unwise political decisions.

Chapter Ten

Nothing Fails Like Success

The initial success of the Zionist project in the 20th century was extraordinary. Yet Israeli political behavior reflected the admonition of management guru Peter Drucker that "nothing fails like success". Drucker felt that success often bred a mentality of smug satisfaction; an attitude that often inured successful people from recognizing threats and dangers as well as new and previously unimagined opportunities and prospects; an attitude that eventually led to failure which was sometimes catastrophic. The history of the Zionist project reflected Drucker's admonition. By any objective standard the Zionist project – the State of Israel – was one of the most successful endeavors in human history. But in its very success lay the seeds of its own self-destruction. An early indicator of this was how the success of the 6-Day War led to the debacle of the Yom Kippur War.

The aims of Zionism had been to create a Jewish state, concentrate a majority of the Jewish People within that state, integrate peacefully into the Middle East, achieve relative economic independence and build a model society. By the first decades of the 21st century, Zionism had established a state which, despite Arab hostility, had become part of the world community. Israel had become the largest Jewish community in the world and by 2025 contained more Jews than the entire Diaspora. It had created a vital and highly developed economy despite what some researchers estimated as 44 billion dollars of economic harm caused by the Arab Boycott since its establishment. It had also been slowly integrating into the region since the 1979 peace treaty with Egypt (*despite* intifadas and wars and 'Arab Springs').

Political Achievements

By 2014, the vision of creating a model society had retreated somewhat in the face of the hard reality of human nature. Yet Israel's political achievements were still historic. In 2014 only 22 countries had been continuously democratic since 1948 when Israel was established. They included: Austria, Australia, Belgium, Canada, Costa Rica, Denmark, Finland, Germany, Iceland, Ireland, Israel, Italy, Japan, Luxembourg, Netherlands, New Zealand, Norway, Sweden, Switzerland, United Kingdom and the United States.

That Israel was even included in this 'Club of 22' is extraordinary. Israel achieved democratic maturity and created a constitutional tradition faster than any other society in human history and did so during a War of Independence in which it was fighting for its very existence. It absorbed millions of immigrants, most of whom came from countries with no democratic traditions. It created a functioning parliamentary system with serious working committees and, despite its often boisterous behavior, a parliamentary etiquette in which even Arab MK's who were enemies of the very idea of a Jewish State had freedom of speech and often presided as acting Speakers of the Knesset. Israel was also the only former colony, mandate or protectorate ruled by an imperial power included in the 'Club 22' and the only democratic country in history that had been in a formal state of war, with all the constitutional dilemmas that implies, since its founding. Israel's democratic and constitutional evolution was one of the most amazing achievements in the political history of the human race.

Constitutionalist evolution had been ongoing. Oriental Jewish music, cultural expression and food had moved from the margins into the mainstream. The status of women, while still lagging behind Scandinavia, was probably equal to the USA and more than a match for France, Germany and Italy at the time. By 2012, gay rights and cultural acceptance were amongst the most advanced in the world. For a country that fashionable public opinion at the time considered so 'flawed', these were truly extraordinary achievements.

The founding of the United States as a constitutional democracy has often been called "the miracle in Philadelphia". Yet the American founding fathers were products of three preparatory traditions: the British constitutional tradition going back to the Magna Carta (1215), through to the Petition of Right (1628), and the English Bill of Rights (1689); the European Enlightenment tradition with its stress on the freedom and dignity of the individual as well as religious tolerance; and the colonial tradition of self-government. Historians have termed the 13 colonies: "13 schools of self-government". All 13 had been de facto self-governing constitutional republics for decades before the War of Independence. By 1776, Virginia and Massachusetts, the two major players in the revolution against Britain, had been self-governing for a longer period of time than had elapsed from the American Civil War to 2012. The youngest colony, Georgia, had been self-governing for a longer period of time than half the member countries of the United Nations in 2012. The founding fathers of the United States were preeminently prepared, like no other group of men in history, for the experiment in democratic self-government.

The real miracle was "the miracle in Tel Aviv": A group of men and women from such outposts of political "enlightenment" and "democratic" tradition as Pinsk, Warsaw, Moscow, and Baghdad, three years after the Holocaust and surrounded by millions of enemies threatening to exterminate them, created a robust constitutional democracy with more systemic stability than that great revolutionary icon France. Moreover, this was not a static stability; it was a vigorous evolving stability with constantly expanding constitutional protections and cultural broadmindedness. For while there was still structural discrimination and cultural prejudice against minorities – as there was in every other country in the world – there was no official legal or constitutional discrimination and the progress of rights for Israel's Arab citizens had been constant and substantive; this despite Israel having been at war with the Arab world since its inception. The branding of Israel as an Apartheid state by the Left drove Israelis to distraction and generated a psychology amenable to the settler argument that "the whole world is against us", no matter what we do.

Diplomatic Achievements

Israel's diplomatic achievements had been no less impressive. Sadat's visit to Jerusalem and the peace agreement with Egypt, the Madrid conference and the much (unjustly) maligned Oslo Agreements with the Palestinians, as well as the subsequent peace agreement with Jordan and de-facto relations with Morocco and some Gulf States represented Zionism's greatest triumph since the creation of the State of Israel. This was because there had been an essential asymmetry between Arab and Zionist strategy following the creation of the state. Zionist strategy strove for Israel's peaceful integration into the region while Arab strategy strove to drive the Jews out of the region. The peace process, as flawed as it was, was an unstated Arab admission that their strategy had failed and Zionism's strategy had succeeded.

This would have remained the case no matter what the fate of the peace process following the Second Intifada, the Second Lebanese War, the 'Arab Spring' or any other future crisis. What had been done could not be undone, no matter how hard radical Islamists and Arab nationalists (and some Jews) tried. They could not deny that they had sat with the Israelis in the same room, negotiated and signed peace treaties with them, conducted economic activity with them and made their own initiatives regarding a comprehensive settlement. Nor could they have reversed other consequences of these developments, such as Israel's improved relationship with the rising powers of China and India which, previous to Oslo, had been hindered because of these countries identification with the Arab cause. Even something as extreme as Egypt and Jordan revoking their treaties with Israel would not and could not have caused China and India to revert to a position of *status quo ante* regarding their relationship with Israel.

Economic Achievements

These political developments had direct positive consequences for Israel's economic health. Israel was a small country (about the size of New Jersey or Massachusetts in its pre-1967 borders) and completely dependent on exports. From 1991 (the Madrid Conference) to 2000 (the outbreak

of the Second Intifada) 60% of the growth in Israel's exports
were to countries with which it did not have full diplomatic
and economic relations before 1991. This included China
and India, which resumed diplomatic relations with Israel
in 1992. Because of this, by 2014 Asia became Israel's second
largest trading partner, after the EU and before the United
States. Between the end of World War II and 2012, some 70
new states had gained independence, including the State of
Israel. By 2012, among those 70 states Israel's economy was
ranked second, after Singapore,.

Israel's economy grew by 40% in the 90's and it became a world
class high-tech center and came to be known as *Silicon Wadi*.
This enabled it to absorb over one million new immigrants,
mostly from the former Soviet Union. These immigrants
supplied Israel with about 50% of its technical and scientific
manpower during this period, without which they could
not have become *Silicon Wadi*. *Silicon Wadi* was to a large
extent created by the Russian immigration which enabled it
to absorb the Russian immigration. In addition, along with
natural increase, this immigration increased the Jewish
population of Israel by 25% and the non-religious Jewish
population by 40%, thereby mitigating, at least temporarily,
the developing demographic time bomb.

This is why the peace process was a Zionist asset in and of
itself. The fact that Israel's Jewish voters did not appreciate the
historic contribution of the admittedly flawed peace process

to these developments was attributable to the intellectual shallowness of Israel's political class – Left and Right. The Left attributing the terrorist attacks following Oslo to Israeli intransigence completely alienated the Israeli public from the peace process itself and eventually effectively destroyed the Zionist Left parties. The nationalist and religious right-wing parties shamelessly exploited the fears and residual paranoia of the Jewish population to completely discredit the peace process per se. Its sponsors were branded "Oslo Criminals" and Prime Minister Yitzhak Rabin was assassinated because of subsequent incitement against them.

As a consequence of its economic achievements, Israel had ceased to be dependent on Jewish philanthropy, German reparations and American aid, and could have survived without any of it for the first time in the history of the Zionist enterprise – in other words threats to Israeli policy by withholding aid were no longer viable. This was an outstanding accomplishment given the challenges Israel faced. Many Diaspora Jews as well as non-Jews (and even many Israelis) were under the mistaken impression that Israel would still not be able to survive without American aid or Diaspora contributions. The truth is that by 2012, funds raised for Israel by *all* Diaspora Jewish organizations combined represented less than a half a percent of Israel's GDP, while American aid represented about 1.2% of Israel's GDP. These percentages declined every subsequent year.

In 2006, only 120 million dollars of American aid was targeted for civilian purposes. It was the last year Israel received any civilian aid. In contrast, before the election of Hamas, the United States had been giving the Palestinian Authority 350 million dollars a year. All American aid to Israel subsequent to 2006 was military and totaled about two to three billion dollars a year. This was much less than the 40-50 billion dollars a year the American military spent on defending Persian Gulf countries between the two Iraq wars. The military aid provided by the United States to the Muslim Gulf States totaled over a half a trillion dollars between the two Iraq wars. The military aid given to Israel during the same period was between 25-30 billion dollars. The difference was how both were itemized in the American budget. Israel's was listed as foreign aid, while aid to the Gulf States' was reflected in America's own military budget. America's NATO contribution also had not been listed as foreign military aid to Europe, nor was the money that tens of thousands of American troops poured into the local economies of these countries listed as foreign civilian aid, even though Germany's economic miracle following WWII was attributable in some measure to both.

Moreover, most of America's military aid never came to Israel and had no economic impact on the local economy (unlike the positive economic impact of the American troop presence on local economies in Europe and in the Persian Gulf). 75% of American military aid to Israel was deposited in American banks and used to buy American military supplies (generating jobs for an estimated 40,000 American families). 25% of the military aid was discretionary and did come directly to Israel. This was usually used to finance research and development of arms systems, such as the Arrow anti-missile missile, which Israel could carry out more efficiently than the United States (with subsequent savings to the American taxpayer).

Israel was also a major provider of much of America's human intelligence about the Middle East. The militarily relationship was much less one-sided than was generally perceived and of minor importance to Israel's *economic* wellbeing. Compared to the trillions of dollars of indirect military aid given to Europe and Japan during the Cold War by way of the stationing of hundreds of thousands of American troops and powerful naval fleets, American aid to Israel was a bargain – especially as it was the only military aid America gave to any of its allies that did not entail the stationing of American troops. That Israel did not make PR hay of these facts cost it dearly in public opinion.

The threat to stop military aid as a means to pressure Israel into following risky policies became obsolete in the first decade of the 21st century. This was recognized by most sophisticated policy makers in the United States and Europe. They realized that Israel could now manage its security without such aid but also know that any arbitrary moves would make Israel more stubborn, not more flexible. They also knew that a possible reaction might be to make its implicit nuclear capability explicit. This would almost certainly leave limited room for diplomatic maneuver and inflame the area even more. In Grand Strategic terms Israel had never been more secure, yet it's increasingly right-wing leaders exaggerated its security problems making its citizens feel evermore insecure – all for political advantage.

Scientific and Cultural Achievements

In the ten years between 1993 and 2003, Israel's scientific publications per capita were third out of 39 countries, after Switzerland and Sweden. In 2007 the 'Red Herring Index' ranked the outstanding start-ups in Europe: 10 out of the top 100 outstanding companies were Israeli. Israel was ranked 4th in all of Europe. Britain had 24, Germany 14 and France 13. Israel had more outstanding start-ups than Ireland, Switzerland, Holland, Italy, Norway and Spain combined.

Israel was one of eight countries that had developed their own communications satellites as well as the ability to launch them. The other seven were the United States, Russia, France, Britain, Japan, India, and China. Moreover, while these countries launched to the east, utilizing the extra energy derived from the earth's rotation, Israel was forced by geopolitical considerations to launch westward. This forced Israel to make its satellites much smaller. By 2012 this had made Israel the leader in satellite miniaturization with the best weight/performance ratio in the world.

Technological capability developed in Israel led to several important collaborations with leading international bodies. One was the French Space Agency (CNES) with whom Israel was developing a scientific observation satellite based mainly on Israeli technology. In 2004 Israel joined the prestigious *Galileo Project* to set up a global satellite array to provide accurate time and place location with a budget of over 3.5 billion Euros to offer an alternative to the monopoly of the GPS system. Israel had invested only 20 million Euros in the program and this enabled it to become only the second country outside Europe to join the project after China. Over and above the tactical and strategic advantages of this involvement, Israel's space industry served as a technology engine carrying a number of other industries along with it.

By 2014 Israel was poised to become a world leader in clean-tech as it had become in hi-tech. Israel was a world leader in recycling 75% of its sewage waste water. Spain, in second place, recycled only 12%. Israel introduced the world to revolutionary drip irrigation which utilized 70%-80% of the water as opposed to 40% with ordinary irrigation methods. The agricultural yield per unit of water in Israel had become the highest in the world. Aggregate water consumption in Israel had not grown in the 40 years prior to 2012 despite a considerable growth in population, agricultural production and industrial development. In other words water consumption per individual citizen had plummeted with no sacrifice to either hygiene or the economy. The largest and most advanced desalination installation in the world had been built in Ashkelon and was capable of producing the cheapest desalinated water in the world. It was built in cooperation with large French firm desalination, which by 2014 had invested over one billion dollars in Israel. Israel's political relationship with France might have been difficult, but it's scientific, technological and business relationship was second to none.

Israel was the only country in the world that began the 21st century with a larger number of trees than it had in 20th century. Israel had a lower infant mortality rate than the average in the OECD countries. Life expectancy in Israel was higher than average for OECD countries. Moreover, the necessary tasks of the Zionist enterprise contributed to universal human civilization. Following are only two:

- The Zionist success in reviving the Hebrew language (one of the greatest achievements of Zionism) became a 'light unto many nations'. The Welsh, Scots, Irish, Dutch as well as Azerbaijan, Brittany, Catalonia and New Zealand all used the *Ulpan* system either to teach new immigrants the language of their new country or to renew their own native languages.

- The Zionist success in creating a modern society in an arid ecology was also a 'light unto many nations'. Israeli foresters were asked to oversee and advise massive arid zone reforestation projects in countries as diverse as Mexico and China. Israeli water engineers and agronomists advised developing *and developed* countries world over.

Israel had succeeded in becoming an independent country making vital contributions to all of humanity, a triumph of human energy, will and perseverance. This tremendous success blinded its leaders and most of its citizenry to the limits of power as well as the socio-cultural constraints of the 21st century with dreadful consequences. The declining impact of the Arab boycott; the opening of formerly closed world markets; the legitimization of Israel as an object of international investment and the continued growth of the Israeli economy would have more than made up for the end of Jewish and American aid. Ending the false sense of security American aid provided Israel might even have compelled organizational and administrative efficiencies that would have been beneficial to the Israeli economy in the long run. Unfortunately Israel, with the kneejerk backing of American Jewry, did not forgo this easy money, which did not require them to implement efficiencies or change fundamental policy towards the settlers and the ultra-Orthodox. Israel slowly sunk into a fetid swamp of mediocrity that completely neutralized the potential of Silicon Wadi. Israeli politicians, Jewish lay leaders and professionals in the 21st century exhibited a bankruptcy of imagination and energy that prevented the Zionist project from rising to Jabotinsky's third stage of Zionism enabling it to implement Ben Gurion's vision of Israel becoming "a light unto the nations".

Chapter Eleven

The Special Case of American Jewry

Israelis had never come to terms with the fact that in regards to the so-called 'Jewish question' America was different and American Jewry was different. American Jews, while for the most part robustly supportive of Israel, were indifferent to fundamental Zionist arguments and not impressed with Israeli intellectuals and politicians preaching the classic Zionist message. Unlike 19th century European Jewry, Zionist arguments had little significance for the 20th and 21st century American Jewish experience.

This explains many of the subsequent tensions between Israelis and American Jews, and why they often did not understand one another. America's religious pluralism, and its 'live and let live' cultural attitude backed up by the *First*

Amendment provided fertile soil for internal Jewish pluralism in a way that the Israeli reality had no way of dealing with. The United States is structurally the most secular country in history; is ideologically neutral in regards to choice of religion, yet sociologically is one of the most religious countries in the world. In the United States one's sub-cultural identity is most often determined by one's religious identification or lack thereof – 'secularism' is a default position, not a positive ideology that evangelizes itself in opposition to religion (as in France for example, as well as in Israel).

The American Zionism of Justice Louis Brandeis and American Jewish philosopher Horace Kallen was a more accurate reflection of the American Jewish experience. Unlike classical Zionists, they did not advocate for the negation of the Diaspora – they believed that Zionism would strengthen the American Diaspora; that the creation of Israel would imbue American Jews with more self-confidence and self-esteem and thus would make them better *American* citizens. Brandeis believed that: "To be good Americans, we must be better Jews, and to be better Jews, we must become Zionists."[44] Kallen coined the phrase 'cultural pluralism' and defended the 'right to be different.' In this he was but an American iteration of Mazzini's *Romantic Nationalism*. As Dr. Sarah Schmidt put it "Kallen learned to overcome his 'dumb anxiety' over his Jewish identity by 'living and orchestrating it' with the principles of the American Idea, individual liberty and freedom." This enabled Kallen to become "one of the first active American Zionists, a founder of the American Jewish Congress ... and a behind-the scenes force in defining the direction of much of American Jewish communal life..."[45] Looking at the status of Jews in American society before and after the creation of the State of Israel one would be hard put to deny the validity of Brandeis and Kallen's position.

What was so singular about America that made it less amenable to the classic Zionist call to negate the Diaspora? At the most fundamental level it was because America's history, cultural origins and foundational mythologies were different from those of Europe. The United States was the only Western country whose mythologies were, as Kallen had indicated, Old Testament and not pagan. The Bible and biblical metaphor formed the foundation of American culture, not the Greco/Roman, Teutonic or Druidic myths which reflect the pagan roots of European culture. Exodus and the search for the *Promised Land* was the dominant American metaphor. America had transformed the idea of the *Promised Land* into an amorphous concept called *The American Dream*. The Exodus metaphor appears in various degrees in all five of the foundational cultures of the United States: the Pilgrims and Puritans, African Americans, the West, the mass immigration, and suburbia.

Pilgrims and Puritans

The metaphor of both Pilgrims and Puritans was Hebrew. England was their Egypt and the King their Pharaoh. The

Atlantic Ocean was their Red Sea and America the New Canaan. America's Puritan heritage and other fundamental Protestant influences have engraved the American character with the Hebrew imprint. American mythology is Old Testament. Neither Thor nor Jupiter lies at the bottom of the American character, but Moses, the Chosen People, the Promised Land, and redemption. The Puritans saw their religion as a continuation of the Covenant of Israel but under a different administration. This is a fundamental cultural genome of American 'Exceptionalism'.

One message of the Old Testament was that a nation as well as an individual could be in covenant with God. The Pilgrims intended to establish such a nation, doing God's work, on the shores of the New Canaan of America. This vision still has enormous impact on the American character and partially explains that sense of exceptionality that Americans have about themselves (which so often infuriates other nations). Many early Americans found justification for their distaste for Absolutism and Divine Right in the Old Testament. They believed that government must be moral before it is political. The equal protection clause of the Constitution has its roots in the belief that all men are equal in the eyes of God.

The infatuation of the Jews with America equaled that of the Protestant Americans with the Hebrew heritage. Early Sephardic Jews, in an attempt to identify America with the Promised Land, asserted that the American Indians were descendants of the Ten Lost Tribes. Ashkenazi Jews called America *Die Goldene Medina*—'the golden country' (*The Land of Milk and Honey*). The word *America* quickened the hearts of Jews for years, in ways only surpassed by the word Israel. Revolutionary America and modern Israel were also strikingly similar. They were the only countries in the world to be designed as a country, a society, and a culture, by a group of founding fathers inspired by visions of a universal role. The Messianic prophetic message informed both, for better and worse. It was this cultural infrastructure that gave the American iteration of Christian Zionism its particular force.

African Americans

The second foundational culture was that of the African Americans. It was also based on the Exodus metaphor, although in both negative and positive ways. It was both an escape from the Egypt of America and a journey to the promised land of America. The Black spirituals, rooted as they were in the slave experience, sang of deliverance from slavery, going into the Promised Land (*Go Down Moses*), and crossing the river Jordan (the Mississippi serving as a substitute — how water-deprived Israelis wished it were so!). Examine the speeches of Martin Luther King and other Black civil rights leaders and see how often the Exodus and redemption metaphors repeated themselves. In King's last speech the day before he was murdered, he likened himself to Moses standing on Mount Nebo and looking out over the Promised Land that God was giving to the Israelites:

... I've been to the mountaintop ... I just want to do God's will. And He's allowed me to go up to the mountain. And I've looked over. And I've seen the Promised Land. I may not get there with you. But I want you to know tonight, that we, as a people will get to the Promised Land. And I'm happy, tonight. I'm not worried about anything. I'm not fearing any man. Mine eyes have seen the glory of the coming of the Lord.

The Saga of the West

The great migration to and conquest of the West was another great Exodus. The West with all that it represents (cowboys, individualism, and freedom) became a fundamental saga of American culture. Those pioneers were looking for their own promised land. They wanted to leave the perceived injustices of the East for freedom, dignity, and happiness. Read the correspondence and the diaries of these pioneers and you will discover redemptive biblical language in its full force. James Michener's popular novel *Centennial* captured the sense of destiny of these pioneers. Prayers of guidance and of thanksgiving were their daily lot. The phrase *Manifest Destiny* connotes a God-given right and task, similar to the God-given right and duty of the Israelites to conquer the Promised Land. American politicians spoke about the God-given rights of the God-fearing nation to these lands. Native Americans were sometimes seen as hostile *Canaanites* who had to be eliminated to make room for God's people. To justify their eradication the white settlers often called them *Amalek*.

The Immigrant Saga

The immigrant saga is the fourth foundation of American culture. America was the Promised Land for a mixed multitude of downtrodden peoples looking to escape the persecutions of modern day Pharaohs and find freedom and dignity. Their Exodus was in steerage, not on camel or donkey, and the ocean, as with the Pilgrims, was their Sinai wilderness. Their sighting the Statue of Liberty at the gateway to the Promised Land after their travails remind one of the Israelites looking over the Jordan River from Mount Nebo into their Promised Land after forty years in the desert.

Suburbia

The foundation cultures of the Puritans, African-Americans, the West, and mass immigration are all variations of the Exodus metaphor. In addition, we have the materialistic redemption dream of suburbia, a caricature of the Exodus metaphor, but no less powerful than the other foundation cultures in molding the American persona. Fleeing the imperfect city — looking for the American Dream of perfect happiness and harmony in the Promised Land of new perfectly designed communities.

American Culture and American Patriotism

Europeans often derided the United States for having no culture. This was both true and untrue. The United States certainly had culture and profound cultural creativity. But unlike Europe, America had no generally agreed upon normative culture. It was a mosaic of subcultures. American cultural life had no center and no periphery. Neither Jews nor anyone else could be accused of not assimilating, like the Eastern European Jews in Germany, or assimilating too much, like Stalin's 'rootless cosmopolitans' in the Soviet Union. Could anything have been more amenable for Jews than this?

Patriotism in the United States was also different. It was not measured by swearing loyalty to Volk, Fatherland, or hereditary sovereign; it was measured by swearing to uphold and defend the Constitution. Civil rules of behavior, not race, blood, or mythical appeals to the land and historical legend determined what a true American was. One did not pledge allegiance to the tribe; one pledged allegiance to the flag and 'the Republic for which it stands': that is, to the Constitution, which is the Republic. A true American was one who adhered to Americanism, to the American way of life, not to particular bloodlines. This is why ethnic Chinese, Italians, *and Jews* could talk about 'our Pilgrim forefathers' without any sense of absurdity.

Is it any wonder then that few other ethnic groups in the United States had surpassed the Jews in believing in or taking advantage of and fulfilling the American Dream? Judged by the practical standards of Americanism, the Jews were the most American of all the American ethnic groups.

They were the wealthiest, best educated, most professional, most organized ethnic group in the United States. They had a higher percentage of political representatives in proportion to their size than other minorities—even representing areas that had no sizable Jewish vote. Over 90% of eligible Jewish voters voted; much higher than any other demographic group in the United States – even the so-called 'real Americans.'

Yet with all these achievements in retrospect we see that late 20th century and early 21st century organized American Jewry behaved in ways that were dysfunctional to the political and cultural health of Israel and, as a consequence, to their own social and cultural health. Their unconditional support for every Israeli government and every Israeli policy increasingly alienated growing numbers of Jews not identified with Jewish organizations, who drifted slowly but steadily away from support or even empathy for Israel. American Jewry could have been the poster child for the truism that "nothing fails like success". These failings, and their ultimate catastrophic consequences, will be examined in a subsequent chapter.

PART II – RESENTMENT
AND BAD POLICY

Resentment is a much ignored factor in the study of history. Consider how history might have changed if George Washington's fellow British officers had treated him and his Virginia militiamen with respect during the *French and Indian War*, instead of dismissing them as just "Americans" (at the time an insult). Would this most English of Englishmen have become a revolutionary and the 'father' of the new country? What would have been the political disposition of Middle Eastern Jews if they hadn't resented the way they were treated by the left-wing Israeli establishment when they immigrated to Israel? Or their resentment towards left-wing Israeli intellectuals who lectured them that Arab and Muslim anti-Jewish attitudes were of no consequence and that if Israel only gave up the conquered territories and established a Palestinian State these attitudes would vanish and Israel would be accepted in the Middle East? Or the resentment of traditional Israelis of all ethnic backgrounds regarding perceived western indifference to the special affinity Jews had to the Land of Israel; or the Palestinians disallowing that the Jews even had a unique historical and cultural attachment to the land? The chronic resentment of large portions of the Jewish population spilled over into political discourse and policy making and caused the Jews to make political decisions based on indignation, which in retrospect can now be seen as ruinous.

The denial of Israel's very right to exist by large segments of the so-called 'progressive' Left stimulated resentment on steroids. As previously mentioned Italy's descent into Fascism did not call into doubt the right of the very existence of the Italian state; unlike Israel for which many more minor transgressions the rights of the very existence of the Jewish state were called into question. The Armenian genocide was an outrage that never resulted in questioning the very right of the Turks to have their own Turkish state, even when the Turks continued to deny that it even happened. Even the Nazi era did not call into question the legitimacy of the existence of the German state.

Such double standards contributed to the general resentment of the Israeli electorate, making them immune to even justifiable and constructive criticism. The campaign to delegitimize the very existence of the Jewish state was unprecedented in modern history, and Israelis came to view this fanatic anti-Zionism as the postmodern iteration of anti-Semitism. This had unintended and negative consequences – all criticism of Israel came to be viewed as anti-Semitism and thus Israel slowly became deprived of the healthy role that criticism plays in a robust democratic society. Israel's political culture became weakened. The resentment of Israelis regarding their delegitimization became the dominant psycho-political characteristic of Israeli society. The consequences for the Zionist project were disastrous.

Chapter Twelve

The World's Double Standard

One of the explanations for Israel's irrational policy decisions was the accumulated resentment many Israelis felt regarding the perceived unfair mindset of much of world opinion and policy. Israelis often viewed themselves as victims of a chronic double standard. Critics of Israel saw this as whining self-pity, but objective research reveals that the double standard was real. Ironically, Israeli self-criticism was often more robust than Israel's critics in the United States or Europe; it was certainly more vigorous than even the most far-reaching criticism coming from within the American Jewish community. But the world's double standard made it difficult for self-critical Israelis to be heard and thus re-enforced the slide towards irrational policy making that eventually resulted in the demise of the State.

The Refugee Racket

The most prominent example of the double standard was the mindset relating to the Palestinian refugee issue. UN General Assembly resolution 194 (December 1948) calling for the return of Palestinian refugees to their former homes in Israel was actually a *Bill of Attainder*[46]. No similar resolution existed for the 20 million refugees that resulted from the partition of India or for the 9 million ethnic Germans expelled from their ancestral homelands in Eastern Europe following WWII. What is more, actual implementation of UN Resolution 194 (as interpreted by Israel's enemies) would have meant the destruction of the Jewish State. This would have been a violation of the UN Charter declaring the right of all peoples to self-determination. The Palestinians could have achieved self-determination without the so-called 'right of return' to Israel, while its implementation would have deprived the Jews of their right of self-determination. Resolution 194 could, therefore, have been interpreted as unconstitutional on two grounds: 1) it was clearly a *Bill of Attainder*; 2) its implementation would have resulted in the death of a sovereign state thus violating the UN Charter.

Few, if any, Israelis who supported a two-state solution questioned the right of the Palestinians to legislate a '*Law of Return*' (as distinct from a 'right of return') to a sovereign Palestine. However, none but the suicidal would have endorsed a Palestinian 'right of return.' What is more, many settlers and other religious Israelis claimed that they also had a 'right of return' to their ancestral homeland in Judea and Samaria. Given the centrality of the Land of Israel for Jews, this was not a frivolous claim. The response that given the enormous period of time that elapsed since the Roman expulsion of the Jews from the Land of Israel (and their renaming it Palestine after the Philistines) this was no longer pertinent, invited the counter-response that if that were the case, all the settlers had to do was to wait long enough until it was no longer pertinent for the Palestinians. All in all, the so called 'right of return' (which appears nowhere in international law) was one of the most formidable obstacles to achieving peace and served no useful moral or practical purpose.

The very existence of UNRWA could also have been seen as a *Bill of Attainder*. The Palestinian refugee question was the ONLY refugee issue with its own UN agency. Every other refugee problem was handled by UNHCR – *The United Nations High Commission on Refugees*. Even more bizarre, UNRWA defined Palestinian refugees as persons who lost home and livelihood as a result of the 1948 conflict, *as well as their descendants*. Palestinians were, therefore, the only group in the world whose descendents could *inherit* refugee status from parents and grandparents. By this standard, every Jew in the world would be considered a refugee. Using this definition, UNRWA estimated that in 2012 there were 5 million Palestinian refugees – only 50,000 of which were original living refugees from the 1948 Israeli War of

Independence. The UNRWA definition was made in-house by UNRWA bureaucrats and had no standing in international law or any international protocols or conventions on refugees, yet was treated with almost holy deference by the western interlocutors of the peace process – a double standard that absolutely infuriated Israelis. If this standard had been applied to the descendants of those displaced during the partition of India there would have been over 100 million refugees in 2014. UNHCR, on the other hand defined refugees as follows:

> A 'refugee' is a person who owing to a well-founded fear of being persecuted for reasons of race, religion, nationality, membership of a particular social group, or political opinion, is outside the country of their nationality, and is unable to or, owing to such fear, is unwilling to avail him/herself of the protection of that country.[47]

International law designates refugees as persons compelled by circumstances to leave their country of origin while not receiving citizenship in another country. Descendents and individuals who have received citizenship from another country are not refugees under International Law (let alone common sense). Descendents of refugees who have not received citizenship from another country are considered stateless persons under International Law – not refugees. When Israelis pointed out that the very existence of UNRWA was discriminatory they were accused of putting obstacles in the path of peace. The substantial Arab immigration to Palestine in the 20s and 30s, attracted by economic opportunities created by Zionist development policies, was not even a subject for discussion.[48]

The Palestinian 'refugee problem' had become an international fetish to the detriment of other refugee and human rights problems. For example, primarily Buddhist Bhutan had been engaging in meticulous and planned ethnic cleansing of its Hindu Nepalese minorities for over 20 years with next to no international condemnation. From 1991 until 2012 Bhutan had generated the highest numbers of refugees in the world in proportion to its population; over one sixth of Bhutan's population had sought asylum in Nepal, India and other countries around the world. Over 105,000 Bhutanese had been living for more than 15 years in refugee camps established in Nepal by the *United Nations High Commission for Refugees*. By 2014, tens of thousands of these refugees had been re-settled in the USA, Canada, Australia, Denmark, New Zealand, the Netherlands, the UK and Norway.[49]

The United States alone had absorbed over 66,000 Bhutanese refugees by 2013 while in aggregate other countries had absorbed approximately 12,000; in total 70% of the refugees. Imagine if a proportional effort had been made in 1950 regarding the original 711,000 Palestinian refugees and over 500,000 were resettled in an organized fashion in various Western and Arab countries. Imagine if a separate refugee organization (UNRWA), having a vested professional interest in sustaining the 'problem', had not been established and the Palestinian refugees had been dealt with by the UNHCR whose mission (and track record) was to actually resolve refugee problems rather than protract them.

Despite the fact it had been exposed in the *New York Times* and *The Atlantic* as well as other media outlets, the Bhutanese refugee problem was never made a serious public issue by international human rights organizations or the United Nations or the Durban conference. If you had taken a street poll in 2014 in any western nation, 999 out of a thousand would not even have heard of it while the entire thousand would have heard of the Palestinian refugee problem. Not only did the democratic world not make an issue of it, they took it upon themselves to mitigate it by opening their doors for the resettlement of these refugees in their own countries. The fact that the democratic world took upon itself the responsibility of resolving this refugee problem by resettling them in their countries while recognizing the legitimacy of the Palestinian claim to the 'right of return' was not lost on Israeli public opinion.

The Bhutanese refugee problem was only a drop in the bucket of the global refugee problem. According to the American Refugee Committee, in 2012 there were 16 million refugees and 51 million displaced persons worldwide[50], yet in aggregate none of these received even a fraction of the newsprint or public attention given to the Palestinians. The UNRWA budget for 2012 was $907,907,371. It had 29,000 employees serving approximately 1.4 million Palestinians living in 58 refugee camps. Most of the remaining 3.6 million Palestinian so-called 'refugees' received no aid from UNRWA. In contrast, the UNHCR provided assistance to 34 million refugees, stateless persons and internally displaced persons with a staff of only 7,700 and a budget of 4.3 billion dollars. In other words UNRWA spent five times the amount per refugee than UNHCR and had one employee per 48 refugees as opposed to one employee for 4415 refugees for UNHCR. UNRWA had become the de-facto state of the Palestinian people; providing education, health and development budgets, as well as many career opportunities for professional "humanitarians". In the eyes of many Israelis it had become a bigger obstacle to peace than the settlements and was the preeminent example of the world's double standard.

Even more important, from an *honest* humanitarian viewpoint, the Palestinian question had drowned out international attention to other humanitarian issues. By the second decade of the 21st century, 82% of UN General Assembly emergency meetings had been dedicated to condemning Israel. By exaggerating Palestinian suffering, and by blaming the Jews for it, the UN muffled the cries of those who suffered equally (like the Bhutanese) or on a far larger scale, like the indigenous black population of Sudan — Christians and Muslims alike — who had been the victims of brutal and racist Arab Muslim

170 T s v i   B i s k

regimes in Khartoum. Four million innocent Sudanese men, women and children were slaughtered from 1955 to 2005. Seven million were ethnically cleansed and they became the largest refugee group since World War II. Yet while this tragedy was well known to the public, it attracted nowhere the same United Nations attention as the Palestinian issue. And Israel continued to be attacked as being worse than the Apartheid regime of South Africa by luminaries such as Archbishop Desmond Tutu and celebrities such as Pink Floyd's Roger Waters.

Muslim Apartheid and Imperialism

The irony is that those who suffered most from the UN anti-Israel policy were not the Israelis, but all those people whose suffering the UN ignored or downplayed because the Palestinian issue had sucked all the oxygen out of the humanitarian room. What especially infuriated the Israelis was the de facto tolerance for Arab/Muslim abuse of women, ethnic minorities, religious minorities and homosexuals as well as the Copts in Egypt, the Christians in Iraq and the Baha'is in Iran. The Islamic Republic of Pakistan was a particularly offensive example of this double standard:

> Non-Muslim citizens of the Islamic Republic of Pakistan are treated as separate and unequal citizens in a form of religious apartheid. The Constitution and laws of the land are overwhelmingly preferential to Islam, the State Religion, and Muslims. Systematic exclusion of Hindus and

other minorities ranges from humiliations such that a non-Muslim lawyer cannot appear before Federal Shariat Court to Constitutional provisions that the President and Prime Minister of Pakistan must be Muslims. Religious extremism and fanaticism sponsored by the State that disenfranchise its own minority populations have engendered fringe factions that endanger the wellbeing and lives of minorities, including Hindus, Sikhs, Christians, Ahmadiyas, and Shias.[51]

Israelis knew that Sunni Muslims were treated better in Israel than in Iran; that Shiite Muslims were treated better in Israel than in Pakistan and Egypt; that Ahmadi, Sufi and Ismailia Muslims were treated better in Israel than anywhere in the Muslim world; that Muslim women were treated better in Israel than anywhere else in the Muslim world. The double standard was so clearly apparent that it blinded their reason and enabled many Israelis to justify their own self-damaging policies.

Muslim on Muslim violence since WWII was totally ignored. In 2006 Israeli journalist Ben Dror Yemini wrote an essay highlighting the double standard of the world in this regard.[52] According to him, 8.5 million Muslims were killed by their fellow Muslims during this period as compared to one million Muslims killed by USSR/Russia in Afghanistan and Chechnya, 500,000 by France in Algeria and elsewhere, 70,000 by the United States in Iraq and Afghanistan[53] and 60,000 by Israel in ALL of its wars and the occupation. This is not counting the 2.5 million non-Muslims slaughtered by Muslims (total killed by Muslims – over 11 million).

Following is a partial account of the body count. About three million non-Muslims and Muslims slaughtered by Muslims in Sudan. Over a million Muslims killed by fellow Muslims in Afghanistan and another million Muslims killed by the Soviets. In Somalia over 500,000 Muslims were killed by fellow Muslims. Up to 2 million East Pakistanis (Bangladesh) were slaughtered by their West Pakistani fellow Muslims in the 1971 Civil War which also caused 10 million Hindu refugees to pour into India from Pakistan. In 1965-66, the Muslim Indonesian Army slaughtered about 400,000 civilians – Muslims and overseas Chinese, and in 1975-1999 killed up to 200,000 Christians in Timor. In the Iran/Iraq war, three million Muslims were killed by their fellow Muslims. From 1963 to 1970 about 150,000 Muslims were killed in Yemen by Egyptian and Saudi forces. The Russians killed between 100,000 and 300,000 Muslims in Chechnya (adding to their Muslim body count in Afghanistan). Other 'minor' body counts of Muslim killings include: Jordan (up to 25,000 Palestinians killed in Black September by Jordanian Muslims); Chad (30,000 killed by Muslims in civil wars); Tajikistan (50,000 Muslims killed by fellow Muslims in civil war from 1992 to 1996); Syria (father Assad killed 20,000 fellow Muslims in Hama in 1982 and Assad junior killed over 200,000 fellow Muslims and caused millions of refugees in his civil war); Iran killed thousands of opponents and religious minorities after the revolution including 10,000 Kurdish Muslims; Turkey killed over 20,000 Kurdish Muslims; in Zanzibar in the 1960s African Muslims killed up to 17,000 Muslim Arabs; in Nigeria thousands of non-Muslims were killed by Muslim terrorists.

The Marmara flotilla incident was another classic example of the double standard considering Turkey's treatment of their Alevi[54] and Kurdish minorities. Consider also the composition of the Marmara flotilla "activists". No less a personage than Christopher Hitchens – a well known anti-Zionist and critic of Israel – said the following about the "activists" in an interview:

> ... what the people on that flotilla are saying ... and their euphemist supporters are saying, is "we are advance guard of the friends of Hamas and the friends of Jihad," and how they get themselves called activists, I don't really quite know, it's quite clever to get yourself just called that.
>
> If you're a member of a group like International A.N.S.W.E.R... which are the American friends of North Korea, the American friends of Saddam Hussein ... the American defenders of the Islamic republic of Iran, well, they should be brave enough to stand by their principles and not just called that they're activists, and the guests, the honored guests of the thuggish government of Mr. Erdogan, who just a few weeks ago said if anyone mentions the Armenian question in public ever again, I will expel all the remaining Armenians from Turkey. In other words,

don't bring up the last genocide or I'll hurt them again, this man is an out-of-control thug, and he's posing as a defender of the human rights of Palestinians. It makes me want to throw up things I've forgotten ever eating.

The European double standard was seen by many Israelis as indicative of the decay of European civilization resulting from post-colonial guilt morphing into a defeatist political pathology characterized by a decline in moral self-confidence. The rise of the non-western 'rest and mass Muslim immigration into Europe reinforced this political pathology. It led to a pandering to Muslims, characterized by guilt and fear, negating intellectual and moral integrity. In some circles this led to the delegitimization of the Jewish state itself. European post-colonial guilt reflected a profound ignorance of their historical relationship with Islam. Muslim imperialism against Europe preceded the Crusades by several centuries and modern European imperialism by a thousand years. Muslims invaded Spain in 717 and within 8 years conquered the entire Iberian Peninsula. They then invaded France and were only prevented from conquering France by Charles Martel at the battle of Tours in 732. In the 9th century they conquered Sicily and large parts of southern Italy up to Rome. Throughout the 8th and 9th centuries Muslims were conducting raids on Northern Italy and Southern France.

In the 11th century the Normans finally ended Muslim rule in Italy. In a way, the Crusades were but a natural extension of this Christian counterattack against Muslim aggression and not an unprovoked aggression against Islam on the part of the Europeans as modern Muslim apologists often claimed. In Spain, the Christian counterattack known as the *Reconquista* took over seven hundred years until it was completed in 1492 – ironically the Jews became its biggest victims. Muslim aggression against Europe did not stop there. Between 1530 and 1780, over one million Europeans were taken as slaves by Muslim pirates. Professor Robert Davis writes "The fishermen and coastal dwellers of 17th-century Britain lived in terror of being kidnapped by [Muslim] pirates and sold into slavery in North Africa. Hundreds of thousands across Europe met wretched deaths on the Barbary Coast in this way." He expands "In the first half of the 1600s; Barbary ... pirates from ... North Africa, authorized by their governments to attack the shipping of Christian countries, ranged all around Britain's shores ... they grabbed ships and sailors, and sold the sailors into slavery." All of this is well documented. "Admiralty records show that during this time the corsairs plundered British shipping pretty much at will, taking no fewer than 466 vessels between 1609 and 1616, and 27 more vessels from near Plymouth in 1625."[55]

The Ottomans conquered all of the European Balkans and were only stopped at the gates of Vienna. In the 18th and 19th centuries there was continued aggression against European and American merchant marines by the Barbary pirates. Christopher Hitchens wrote an outstanding article about this called "Jefferson Versus the Muslim Pirates" in the spring 2007 edition of the *City Journal,* in which he writes "How many know that perhaps 1.5 million Europeans and Americans were enslaved in Islamic North Africa between 1530 and 1780?" [56] Arab imperialism controlled East Africa in much the same manner as the West controlled China, and the Arab slave trade of black Africans was much more long lived than, and just as cruel as the European Atlantic slave trade. Muslim imperialism conquered all of Southern Asia persecuting Buddhists, Hindus and Zoroastrians. The Hindus despised them as barbarian conquerors.

Yet, by 2014, sympathy towards the Palestinian cause amongst Africans and other people of color in the United States and Europe had become substantial, despite the fact that the Arab Slave Trade both preceded and outlasted the European slave trade. The Arab Slave Trade lasted from 700 to 1911 AD, but slavery itself persisted until 2014. Saudi Arabia and Yemen only abolished slavery in 1962; Oman in 1970 and Mauritania in 1980.[57] During the period of the Arab slave trade, 14 million African slaves were sold while an estimated 14-20 million African men, women and children died. Some Muslim theologians still supported it as late as the 21st century as having Koranic justification. For example, in 2003, Sheikh Saleh Al-Fawzan issued a fatwa that "Slavery is a part of Islam. Slavery is part of jihad, and jihad will remain as long there is Islam." He attacked Muslims who disagreed as being "... ignorant ... Whoever says such things is an infidel." This fatwa was not made by some minor figure. Al-Fawzan was a member of the Senior Council of Clerics, Saudi Arabia's highest religious body, a member of the Council of Religious Edicts and Research, the Imam of Prince Mitaeb Mosque in Riyadh, and a professor at Imam Mohamed Bin Saud Islamic University, the main Wahhabi center of learning in the country. Prominent Saudi cleric, Sheikh Saad Al-Buraik, encouraged Palestinians to capture and enslave Jewish women: 'Their women are yours to take, legitimately. God made them yours. Why don't you enslave their women?'[58]

UN and NGO Hypocrisy

By 2006 the Palestinians had received four times as much aid per Palestinian individual as Europe had received per European individual under the Marshall Plan. UNWRA bureaucrats consistently helped Palestinian politicians misrepresent demographics in order to get more money from the international community. UNRWA had been revealed as a corrupt, inefficient, self-serving and self-perpetuating bureaucracy that had a vested interest in preserving Palestinian suffering numerous times, but continued to receive international support. The irony was the harm done to the Palestinians themselves as a consequence of the forgiving attitude of the international community.

Criticism of Israel from international NGOs such as *The International Committee of the Red Cross* (ICRC), as distinct from the *American* Red Cross, absolutely infuriated Israelis.

It was well documented that the Red Cross had knowledge of the Holocaust and declined to publicize it to the world, claiming that International Law forbade them to do it.[59] This was especially bizarre as the Red Cross publicly accused Israel of crimes against humanity on a regular basis. The Red Cross did not protest when the Swiss State refused to give refuge to Jews fleeing Nazi Germany. The Swiss sent them back to certain death in Germany. The Red Cross sent Swiss physicians to treat Nazi troops on the Eastern front and some ICRC officials aided Nazis to flee to South America after the war and hired Francois Genoud, a notorious Swiss Nazi, to work for them in Belgium after the Holocaust. To see how sordid this individual was, access *Hitler's Swiss Connection*, by David Preston in the *Philadelphia Inquirer* of Jan.1997).[60] Jean-Claude Favez's book *The Red Cross and the Holocaust*, Cambridge University Press, (1999) documented Red Cross involvement with the Holocaust. A survey reviewing the print space devoted to Rwanda, Darfur, and human rights in the Muslim world by *Amnesty* and *Human Rights Watch* reports compared to the print space devoted to Israel and Palestine is instructive in regards to this double standard.

The double standard in regards to the West Bank was especially grating and stood in contradistinction to a larger universal moral principle that is the foundation of democratic civilization – namely equality before the law. Eugene Rostow, former dean of Yale Law School had written:

Legally the West Bank and Gaza Strip are unallocated

parts of the Palestine Mandate ... (and) ... the right of the Jewish People to settle in the West Bank under the Mandate has never been terminated ... Jewish settlement in the West Bank is ... not an intrusion into alien territory ... nor a violation of the Geneva Convention. It is ... (an) exercise of the right protected by Article 80 of the United Nations Charter ...

Israel conquered the West Bank from Jordan, *not from the Palestinians.* Jordan had annexed it in 1948 in contravention of the UN Partition Plan and international law. Only two countries had recognized Jordan's annexation: Great Britain and Pakistan. Yet Jordan's occupation was accepted and granted de facto sanction by the international community because the territory had no official status under international law. Israelis asked if Jordan's occupation and the building of homes and palaces by the Jordanian upper classes in the West Bank after 1948 were legal (or perhaps more accurately, not illegal) under international law, then why was Israel's occupation and building of private middle class residences also not legal under international law. Israel was attacked as a racist apartheid state, yet Jordan before the 6-Day War had not permitted Jews from *anywhere in the world* to visit Jerusalem even to pray at the Western Wall. Jordan was never condemned for their discriminatory occupation of Jerusalem by the UN while Israel, which allowed Muslims from all over the world to come to *Al-Aqsa Mosque,* was repeatedly condemned by the United Nations. The destruction of all the synagogues in Jerusalem as well as turning the Western Wall into a public urinal was also never condemned.

Gaza was different, since Egypt never annexed it. It was, however, an unallocated part of the Mandate that the Egyptians ruled as a military occupier disallowing any local Palestinian autonomy or sovereignty, in non-conformance with UN decisions and international legality. Egypt and Jordan did not respect the human rights of the Palestinians and the international community did not condemn this. The status of the Palestinian refugees in Lebanon was worse than the status of South African Blacks under Apartheid and yet never condemned. Lebanon, Egypt and Jordan were never condemned by United Nations Resolutions for their behavior towards the Palestinians. The UN General Assembly and UNESCO never condemned Jordan for destroying over 40 synagogues and Yeshivas in Jerusalem following the War of Independence while despoiling the Western Wall. In other words, a politically motivated international majority, unconstrained by constitutional limitations of power, decided what was legal or illegal according to political predilection with no reference to objective standards. Moreover, the settlements were never the major obstacle to peace. The Second Intifada broke out after Prime Minister Barak offered a deal to turn 95% of the West Bank and Gaza over to the Palestinians (thereby removing over 100 settlements) while giving the Palestinians sovereignty over land in Israel equivalent to the 5% Israel would have kept in the West Bank and Gaza. The major obstacle to peace was always the Palestinian unwillingness to recognize Israel's historic rights in the Land of Israel in general, and in Jerusalem in particular. While not discounting some of the excesses of Israel's military government over Israeli-Arabs following Israel's War of Independence, it was in no way comparable to the treatment the Jews received in Arab countries.

Chapter Thirteen

Selective History (and Geography)

Selective history, like selective hearing, is a universal disease. The Jews were just as guilty of it as others. But the Palestinians carried it to an entirely new level – not only convincing themselves but most of the world and even large numbers of Jews of extremely dubious 'facts'. This selective history is encapsulated in the Palestinian claim that they have been made to pay for European crimes against the Jews – most notably the Holocaust. Using the Holocaust as 'year one' in the Zionist calendar is quite typical of this selective history. It ignores the fact that Zionism was not a product of the Holocaust, but rather a reaction to the historical treatment of the Jews in Europe *and* the Muslim world well before the Holocaust. As for the Holocaust, the Palestinians 'paid' for a crime they were *prevented* from committing by circumstances.

If Montgomery had not defeated the Germans at *El Alamein* the followers of Haj Amin el-Husseini – the Grand Mufti of Jerusalem and a Nazi supporter – would have assisted them in the extermination of 400,000 Palestinian Jews and then gone on to help purify Egypt of its 300,000 Jews – with Syrian, Lebanese and Iraqi Jewry soon to follow. The Palestinians would have been to Middle Eastern Jews what the Ukrainians were to European Jews – devoted executioners of Nazi policy. How do we know this? Because the Mufti and his followers were quite open and clear about their intentions, if only given the chance.

Moreover, Palestinian pressure on the British to enforce the White Paper probably cost the lives of several hundred thousand European Jews who might have been saved if the British had let them take refuge in what eventually became Israel.[61] The *Farhud* in Iraq in 1941 was a pogrom carried out by pro-Nazi Iraqis actively supported and egged on by the Grand Mufti of Jerusalem[62], the dominant leader of nascent Palestinian Nationalism. It cost the lives of several hundred Jewish men, women and children and was but an extension of the anti-Jewish riots in Palestine instigated by him in 1936 and 1939. This behavior had deep historical roots. As early as 1834 – long before resentment towards Zionism could possibly be used to justify barbaric behavior – local Arabs massacred the Jewish population of Safed.[63] This was not a unique occurrence. Previously, in 1660, local Arabs had slaughtered the Jews of Safed. The claim that Palestinians never persecuted the Jews was patently false.[64]

The claim that Jews were treated better in the Muslim world than in Europe is akin to claiming that Blacks were treated better (or less worse) in Jim Crow Alabama than in Apartheid South Africa is an argument that probably could have been made. But this would not have made Middle Eastern Jews or the American Blacks feel better about the nature of their discrimination. As the orientalist G.E. von Grunebaum wrote, "It would not be difficult to put together the names of a very sizeable number of Jewish subjects or citizens of the Islamic area who have attained to high rank, to power, to great financial influence, to significant and recognized intellectual attainment." However "it would again not be difficult to compile a lengthy list of persecutions, arbitrary confiscations, attempted forced conversions, or pogroms."[65]

The historical Muslim hostility to Jews was ubiquitous from its very beginnings, yet the myth of tolerance of Muslims towards Jews *until* the 'provocation' of Zionism persisted. In the 8th century, Idris the First, the founder of Morocco, wiped out entire communities of Jews in North Africa. In 1066 a mob incited by Muslim preachers destroyed the Jewish quarter of Granada and slaughtered over 4,000 Jews. Jews were forced to live in *Mellahs* (the Muslim analogue to the European Ghetto) in Egypt, Syria, Yemen and Morocco. When the *Almohads* (the medieval analogue to el-Qaeda) conquered Morocco and Islamic Spain in 1172, they forcibly converted, expelled or killed Jews and Christians (much like ISIS in 2014). Some Jews like Maimonides (Rambam) moved to more tolerant parts of the Muslim world while others moved north to Christian areas. The Fez pogrom in 1465 resulted in the slaughter of thousands of Jews. In 1656, the entire Jewish population of Isfahan, Persia (present-day Iran) was expelled from the city. In 1785 hundreds of Libyan Jews were murdered.

The situation of Jews in Arab countries became even more dangerous in the 19th century. Jews in Algeria, Tunisia, Egypt, Libya and Morocco were forced to live in ghettos. In Morocco, Jews were forced to walk barefoot or wear shoes of straw when outside the ghetto. Muslim children threw stones at Jews and harassed them in other ways. The frequency of anti-Jewish violence increased, and many Jews were executed on charges of apostasy. In Algiers, Jews were massacred in 1805, 1815 and 1830. In 1864, pogroms in Morocco killed over 500 Jews. In 1869, 18 Tunisian Jews were killed in Tunis, and on *Djerba* Island an Arab mob looted Jewish homes and stores, and burned synagogues. In 1875, Moroccan Jews were attacked and killed in the streets in broad daylight. In 1897, in present-day Libya, Jews were murdered and their synagogues looted. Ritual murder accusations against the Jews became commonplace in the Ottoman Empire.[66]

The situation of the Jews in Persia (modern Iran) was especially extreme. In 1839 in the city of Meshed, a Muslim mob attacked the Jewish Quarter, burned the synagogue, destroyed the Torah scrolls and forcibly converted the Jews to Islam. Another massacre occurred in Barfurush in 1867. In the 19th century J.J. Benjamin, a Jewish traveler and commentator, wrote about the life of Jews in Muslim Persia thus:

> ... they are obliged to live in a separate part of town ... for they are considered as unclean creatures ... should they enter a street, inhabited by Muslims, they are pelted by boys and mobs with stones and dirt ... they are prohibited to go out when it rains; for it is said the rain would wash dirt off them, which would sully the feet of the Muslims ... If a Jew is recognized as such in the streets, he is subjected to the greatest insults. The passers-by spit in his face, and sometimes beat him ... unmercifully ... If a Jew enters a shop for anything, he is forbidden to inspect the goods ... Should his hand incautiously touch the goods, he must take them at any price the seller chooses to ask for them ... Sometimes the Persians intrude into the dwellings of the Jews and take possession of whatever pleases them. Should the owner make the least opposition in defense of his property, he incurs the danger of atoning for it with his life ... If ... a Jew shows himself in the street during the ... (Muharram)... he is sure to be murdered.[67]

Many were forced to convert to Islam, while others were forced to wear a yellow patch on their clothing to identify them as Jews. Since Iran (literally Land of the Aryans) was not considered a Semitic country by Hitler, some speculate he might have gotten the idea for the yellow star patch from them (just as he expropriated the swastika from the 'Aryan' Hindu tradition). The Jews of Muslim Bukhara in central Asia were also forced to wear yellow clothing in public. Many were forced to convert to Islam. Jews were not the only ones to be 'branded' by Muslims. Christians were also forced to wear special insignia on their clothes. The yellow badge actually originated in 9th-century Baghdad and then spread to medieval Europe; another source of 'inspiration' for the Nazis. Hindus living under Islamic rule in India were also often forced to wear yellow badges, similar to the Jews under Hitler.

In Yemen, Muslims considered Jews to be impure so they were forbidden to touch a Muslim or a Muslim's food and were forced to behave obsequiously to Muslims. They were compelled to walk to the left side of Muslims (next to the hand Muslims used to wipe themselves). Since a Jew could not be higher than a Muslim their dwellings were lower and they were forbidden to ride a camel or horse. They were limited to riding donkeys and even then had to dismount if they approached a Muslim on foot so as not to be higher. Jews were even forbidden by law to defend themselves if attacked by Muslims. [68]

By the 20th century, the status of Jews and Christians in Muslim lands had not significantly improved. H.E.W. Young,

British Vice Consul in Mosul (present-day Iraq), wrote in 1909: "The attitude of the Muslims toward the Christians and the Jews is that of a master towards slaves, whom he treats with a certain lordly tolerance so long as they keep their place. Any sign of pretension to equality is promptly repressed."[69] A majority of Arabs and Muslims supported Nazi Germany and their anti-Jewish policies. Hitler's racial laws of 1935 received praise from all over the Arab world. In 1937 King Saud of Saudi Arabia told an English emissary:

> Our hatred for the Jews dates from God's condemnation of them for their persecution and rejection of Isa (Jesus) and their subsequent rejection of His chosen Prophet (Muhammad) ... for a Muslim to kill a Jew, or for him to be killed by a Jew ensures him an immediate entry into Heaven and into the august presence of God Almighty.[70]

Muslim hatred for the Jews was no doubt inflamed by the creation of Israel but it did not have a virgin birth – the hatred of Jews as Zionists grew upon the fertile field of condescending contempt for any Jewish pretension to equality, which was deeply rooted in Muslim attitudes. Zionism was a Jewish pretension to equality as it pertains to political self-determination. Thus, the so-called Muslim tolerance for Jews was always unequivocally dependent on the Jews recognizing their inferiority of rights (keeping their place) and behaving in an appropriately obsequious manner (much like the Blacks in the Jim Crow American south). For that reason, Middle Eastern Jews were expelled from their historic homelands because they were Jews, and not because they were Zionists (and indeed, most of them were not even Zionists in the modern sense of the word). In 1961, Libyan Jews were deprived of citizenship; followed by Algerian Jews in 1962. Iraq expelled its Jews in 1951, as did Egypt in 1956. Jordanian Law forbade Jews from even living in Jordan; Jordanian Civil Law governing the Jordanian-occupied West Bank stated: "Any man will be a Jordanian subject if he is not Jewish" – *not*, if he is not a Zionist. By contrast, in 2014 there were over 1.5 million Muslim citizens of Israel. From 1948 until the beginning of the 21st century, between 800,000 and 1,000,000 Jews fled, or were expelled from Arab countries. The Jewish communities of the Muslim World were in effect 'disappeared' (in much the same way that South American reformers were later on). While some Jews left for Zionist or economic reasons, most had either been expelled or fled for fear of their lives.

Palestinian Ideology

Overt Palestinian anti-Semitism in league with profound corruption inhibited successive Israeli governments from making decisions that would have been of grand strategic benefit to Israel, and by inference to the entire Jewish people. It was hard for a people that had been so humiliated throughout the ages to accede to the demands of people who had such contempt for them, even when these demands were justified and might have been good for the Jews also. The Hamas Covenant, for example, maintained that the notorious anti-Semitic forgery, *The Protocols of the Elders of Zion*, was authentic and called for the extermination of Israel and the creation of a greater Islamic state in Palestine. It called all Arabs and Moslems that did not adhere to this position, traitors to Allah and implied they were deserving of death. Article 22 was especially embarrassing to the apologists for the Palestinian cause. It revealed the anti-Semitism at the heart of the Palestinian National Movement. There was no way it could be interpreted as anti-Zionism. It contained every canard against the Jews in the canon of anti-Semitism.

With their money, they took control of the world media, news agencies, the press, publishing houses, broadcasting stations, and others. With their money they stirred revolutions in various parts of the world with the purpose of achieving their interests and reaping the fruit therein. They were behind the French Revolution, the Communist Revolution and most of the revolutions we heard and hear about, here and there. With their money they formed secret societies, such as Freemasons, Rotary Clubs, the Lions and others in different parts of the world for the purpose of sabotaging societies and achieving Zionist interests. With their money they were able to control imperialistic countries and instigate them to colonize many countries in order to enable them to exploit their resources and spread corruption there...They were behind World War I, when they were able to destroy the Islamic Caliphate, making financial gains and controlling resources. They obtained the Balfour Declaration, formed the League of

Nations through which they could rule the world. They were behind World War II, through which they made huge financial gains by trading in armaments, and paved the way for the establishment of their state. It was they who instigated the replacement of the League of Nations with the United Nations and the Security Council to enable them to rule the world through them. There is no war going on anywhere, without having their finger in it.

Article 28 contains a lie that Goebbels would have been proud of:

> We should not forget to remind every Moslem that when the Jews conquered the Holy City in 1967, they stood on the threshold of the Aqsa Mosque and proclaimed that "Mohammed is dead, and his descendants are all women"... Israel, Judaism and Jews challenge Islam and the Moslem people. "May the cowards never sleep!"

Examples of the Koranic origins of Moslem anti-Semitism were also contained in the body of the Covenant. For example Article 7 contained the following:

> The Prophet, Allah, bless him and grant him salvation, has said: "The Day of Judgment will not come about until Moslems fight the Jews (killing the Jews), when the Jew will hide behind stones and trees. The stones and trees will say O Moslems, O Abdulla, there is a Jew behind me, come and kill him..."

The moral absolutes of Islam could not tolerate any semblance of Jewish autonomy. Nor could they tolerate the peace process. As article 13 of the Hamas Covenant says:

> Initiatives, and so-called peaceful solutions and international conferences, are in contradiction to the principles of the Islamic Resistance Movement ... There is no solution for the Palestinian question except through Jihad. Initiatives, proposals and international conferences are all a waste of time and vain endeavors.

The original P.L.O. National Covenant, while nowhere as vile in tone as the Hamas one, contained similar contempt for the Jews. And while Arafat had abrogated it on the record[71], most Israelis felt this was only a tactical move and that secretly it was still adhered to by the P.L.O. Unlike much of world opinion, Israelis thought the Palestinians were sincere – that they meant what they said about the Jews and said what they meant – that their utterances were not similar to those of a spoiled brat yelling at his mother that 'I hate you.' Unlike the screaming child, the Palestinians were adults who really did hate the Jews as Jews.

Palestinian Corruption

The extent of corruption in Palestinian governance – whether in the PA or in Hamas – had long been an issue of concern for informed Israeli public opinion. After the Oslo Agreements, the government of Ehud Barak complained to the Clinton administration about this and was told it was none of Israel's

business and that if Israel made a public issue about it
the peace process would be endangered and Israel would
be blamed for that. But the Palestinian street was not so
inhibited. There were demonstrations in Gaza against the
corruption of the Palestinian Authority. Yasser Arafat's genius
was in convincing world opinion that the Second Intifada
was a result of Arik Sharon's provocative visit to the Temple
Mount (the courtyard of the Al Aqsa Mosque) and not a
means of deflecting Palestinian anger from him to Israel
and the occupation. That Israel (Barak approving Sharon's
visit) was stupid in providing Arafat with this justification
is beyond question, but no less a personage than Arafat's
wife, Suha, admitted much later that Arafat had told her
to leave the territories well before Sharon's visit because
he intended to instigate a Second Intifada. Subsequently,
Hamas gained power in Gaza to a great extent as a protest
against PA corruption. Ironically of course their reign was
no cleaner; in 2014 it was estimated that half a dozen Hamas
officials were billionaires and several hundred were multi-
millionaires.

This corruption was well known to the foreign donors (mostly
Europe and the USA) as well as to Israelis, but the foreign
donors rarely even hinted at it publically. They knew that
no matter how great the humanitarian benefit of any project
for the Palestinian people, it would only get done if they not
only paid for it and but also supervised it directly. By 2014,
Palestinian leadership had received more aid per capita than
any other political entity in history. It was estimated that they

had received more than four times the aid per capita than
Europe had received under the Marshall Plan. This money
was not only looted, it was used for political pay-offs to buy
votes and patronage.

Prime Minister Salam Fayyad was respected in the West as a
relatively honest and professional leader who tried to stop the
thievery. But he was politically powerless and the leaders of
Fatah worked endlessly to get rid of him so they could have
unrestricted access to the loot. Hamas also wanted to fire
him. And despite the demands of the Western money donors,
he eventually lost his job. Why didn't the Western funding
stop? Because Western leaders felt that the 'funding' kept
things relatively quiet compared to the rest of the chaos in
the Middle East. In other words the 'funding' was actually
a form of protection money to buy off the neighborhood
thugs. Given this, it was not outrageous that Israeli public
opinion had grave reservations about the potential stability
of any peace agreement with an entity so rife with corruption,
devoid of national institutions and governed by leaders that
more closely resembled Mafia dons rather than statesmen.

Geography Matters

The cavalier attitude of many Western interlocutors towards
Israel's geographical dimensions, when advocating withdrawal
from the 'occupied territories', made them suspect even in
the eyes of many Israeli territorial minimalists. It was if

they were cultivating a purposeful ignorance regarding the significance of territory for defense. For example:

1. Distance from Damascus to Tel Aviv is 133 miles; New York to Baltimore is 170 miles

2. Distance from Damascus to Haifa is 90 miles; New York to Philadelphia is also 90 miles

3. Distance from Tel Aviv to Nablus is 31 miles; from Bronx to Staten Island also 31 miles

4. Distance from Palestinian town of Tulkarm to Israeli city of Natanya is 10 miles; from Bronx to midtown Manhattan is 11 miles.

5. Distance from Gaza city to Ashkelon is 13 miles; from northeast Philadelphia to south Philadelphia is 16 miles.

When rockets were fired from Gaza, residents of Tel Aviv had two minutes to take cover; residents of Ashkelon had about 20 seconds. The claim that in the age of rockets territorial depth meant nothing was either completely ignorant or just plain wickedness. This in combination with the false claims of a Muslim/Jewish Golden Age and the unalloyed evil anti-Jewish language of much Palestinian rhetoric, described above, only worked to strengthen the extreme right-wing of Israeli politics and thus enable the policies that eventually resulted in the self-destruction of the State.

PART III –
INTERNAL WEAKNESSES

Chapter Fourteen

Malfunctioning American Jewry

Mainstream American Jewry bore much of the guilt for the dreadful policy decisions that led to the eventual demise of Israel and subsequently of itself. The organized American Jewish community had significant pretensions regarding modern Jewish history. Some of its intellectuals had developed the two-center theory of Jewish existence in opposition to the one-center theory of Zionism. Most American Jews would have agreed that classical Zionism was right in regard to the rest of the Jewish world but wrong in regard to the United States. The rest of the Jewish world might have been 'in exile', but American Jews were not. They might have put it thus: "We are obviously not in our ancient homeland, but we are still at home". They would claim that the American Jewish relationship to Israel was similar to that of Babylonian Jewry during the Talmudic period and the formation of Rabbinic Jewry. They would claim that modern Jewish life would be able to survive in two equal centers: Israel and North America. Moreover they would claim that the vitality of modern Jewish life actually depended on these two 'vigorous' centers interacting with one another.

This claim would have had much to recommend it if organized American Jewry had indeed developed an independent, self-critical and vigorous Diaspora culture. Instead, they became knee-jerk apologists for Israel and a past-oriented nostalgia center on the one hand, or a morally narcissistic, unvarying critic of Israel on the other hand. American Jewry had produced dozens of museums (mostly of the Holocaust variety) and hundreds of university-based Jewish Studies programs and adult enrichment programs, yet not one serious framework dedicated to formulating robust cultural and organizational alternatives for the future. The *Shoah* became so central to organized Jewish life that Jewish academics seeking research grants or ways to get published joked that "there is no business like *Shoah* business".

There were, of course, many positive developments within American Jewry that were cited by the proponents of the two-center theory as proof of the vigor of the American Jewish community. But in aggregate, American Jewish life had become a vapid caricature of past glories. It had become a museum, a Disneyland of nostalgia for past Jewish cultures with no dynamic future-oriented appeal. Worshipping the past became pathology. Nostalgic *Fiddler on the Roof Judaism* alienated growing numbers of non-orthodox young people more concerned with the future of their own personhood than the past of their peoplehood. As one writer put it:

> Nostalgia might be viewed as a major disease of our time. It reflects a general decadence of cultural creativity into one-dimensional international pop culture or ethnic kitsch. In the Jewish context, this nostalgia industry expresses itself in making Jewish identity a kind of Jewish Disneyland, wherein we create kitsch versions of various aspects of Jewish culture and history: "Hassidland," "Sephardiland," "Litvakland," "Kabbalahland," "Yeminiteland," "Musarland," and so on.

The worldwide wave of nostalgia and publicly funded national folk projects designed to "save our cultural heritage" does not signify a rebirth of ethnic vigor, only ethnic desperation and cultural barrenness. The periodic celebration of ethnicity is not an organic reflection of ethnic roots in one's everyday life; it is rather a vacuous reflection of a chronic sense of emptiness...Jew(s) may at various times and for various reasons utilize particular elements of past ethnic traditions, but this cannot be the backbone of a future-oriented Jewish identity. It is depressingly sunk in the past...as Arthur Lewis, a black intellectual, when refuting the ethnic kitsch of black cultural nationalism, wrote: ". . . only decadent peoples on the way down feel an urgent need to mythologize and live in their past. A vigorous people, on the way up, are more concerned with visions of its *future*."[72]

Given the existential challenges of Israel, a rational division of labor might have dictated that American Jewry take upon itself the task of formulating alternative future-oriented cultural expressions. That they failed to do so is, in hindsight, self-evident. There were just too many fundamental negative trends; trends documented and commented upon in great detail by the American Jewish community itself. These included not only the growing alienation from Israel amongst young Jews but also demographics. For although the Jews had always been a small people and although size has never been a prerequisite to cultural success (witness the tiny populations of Italian Renaissance city-states as well as 18th century Scotland during the Scottish Enlightenment), continued existence is first of all biological and numerical. Below a certain critical mass, even small peoples have difficulty sustaining communal identity and cultural creativity.

In this regard, the long-term statistical trends had become depressing. In the 1990s, the American Jewish Committee's Yearbook reported that American Jewry was shrinking by about ½% a year (in contrast to Israel's Jewish community, which was growing by around 1½ % a year *before Aliyah*). By 2014, Israel had become the largest Jewish community in the world. Other indicators showed that this rate of shrinkage was likely to increase. By the end of the first decade of the

21st century, over half of Diaspora marriages involved a non-Jewish spouse. Some of these resulted in the couple rearing their children as Jews, but most did not.

One of the reasons for the weakened situation of American Jewry at the beginning of the 21st century was that they had never formulated coherent ideologies of Diaspora life in pluralistic constitutionalist societies – their entire existence was in relation to the Jewish State. They were for or against, uncritically supportive or critical, proud of or embarrassed by, or completely ignorant of Israel's political anthropology. Even the pose of indifference to Israel common to a certain portion of American Jewry was a demonstrative indifference – not an indifferent indifference. American Jewry's weakness, therefore, was but a reflection of the diluted image of Israel in the world, as well as in its own eyes. This diluted image was as much the fault of American Jewry as of Israel. American Jewry often turned its back on those articulate young Israelis who had become alienated from the path of Israeli society as well as those young Diaspora Jews who identified with them. This was an exclusionary policy that contributed to the decline of the self-critical vigor of the Zionist project – a historic project that from its very inception was characterized by ruthless self-criticism.

Secular versus Religious

American Jews had great difficulty in coming to terms with the Israeli dichotomy of Religious versus Secular Jews, and the mutual hostility this engendered. They did not understand Orthodox Jewry *being* political parties (rather than *supporting* political parties as in the United States), dedicated to expunging secularism and all heterodox Jewish denominations from Israel's public sphere. Non-Orthodox American Jews often enraged Israeli Jews by complaining about the status of Reform Jews in Israel while making contributions to Orthodox Yeshivas in Israel because of the nostalgia disease. "Oh honey, he reminds me of my grandfather" or "Oh honey, look at the dancing Habadnik". Contributions by Reform and Conservative Jews to Orthodox institutions in Israel were estimated to be double their contributions to Reform and Conservative institutions in Israel. Here the victims were in collusion with those that discriminated against them; a scandalous inconsistency of the first order. Reform Jews for Habad was analogous to the no less ridiculous 'Gays for Palestine' movement (when homosexuality was a crime punishable by death in the Palestinian Authority and Gay Palestinians took refuge in Tel Aviv).

American Jews justified this apparent contradiction by claiming they were contributing to educational institutions and did not want to take part in the politicization of religion that characterized Israeli society. By ignoring the fact that these 'educational' institutions were the political muscle of the various religious parties, they armed those very forces which discriminated against Reform and Conservative Jewry and eventually undermined Israeli democracy and solidarity. Not to mention the content of these 'educational' institutions, many of which taught their students that the Holocaust was God's punishment for the Reform Movement and 'Goyim' (Gentiles) were not truly human.

The obsequiousness of Reform and Conservative Jewry and their spinelessness regarding fighting for their rights deprived Israel of a liberal religious identity as an alternative to Secularism and Orthodoxy. Muslims and Christians had more religious freedom in Israel than Reform and Conservative Jews. Israel did not favor or discriminate against any Muslim or Christian denomination – only against Jewish ones. Catholics, Greek Orthodox and the multiplicity of Protestant denominations were all recognized by the state; Sunni, Shia and the multiplicity of other Muslim denominations (Sufi, Ismailia etc.) were all recognized by the state. But Conservative and Reform Jews were not. Israel discriminated against the largest number of Jews in the world and had become de-facto the most anti-Semitic country in the developed world; thus contributing to its dysfunction.

Jerusalem and Settlements Misunderstood

Radical right-wing American Jews had played a crucial role in the delegitimization of Israel, unnoticed by and uncriticized by mainstream Jewish organizations and leaders. Those Jewish individuals and organizations that did notice and did criticize were disparaged and marginalized by mainstream

Jewish organizations for giving aid and comfort to the Arabs. Not only were their Zionist bona fides questioned, but even their loyalty to the Jewish People. Their fate was similar to the fate of the Zionist Left in Israel – they were bundled with the post-Zionist and anti-Zionist Left and their voices were shut out of mainstream Jewish discourse.

Ignorance played a significant part in the Diaspora discussion about Jerusalem. Few American Jews differentiated between the 'Old City' of Jerusalem – that walled part of the city that contained disputed religious icons of the three monotheistic religions – and East Jerusalem. What they pictured when hearing the phrase East Jerusalem was the Old City, and how could loyal Jews even consider giving that back to the Arabs. Yet East Jerusalem was actually an area east of the walled city, most of which had been annexed to Jerusalem following the 6-Day War. The part that had been annexed was a conglomeration of over 60 impoverished Arab villages and neighborhoods that in the entire 3,000 year history of Jerusalem had never been an integral part of the city. The historical, cultural, religious significance of these villages for the Jewish people was close to nil. Yet, the right-wing propaganda machine had been so effective in sanctifying this so called Jewish "holy ground" that any talk of territorial compromise in this area of Jerusalem, which had never in history been part of Jerusalem, was treated as treason.

The law of unintended consequences always seems to 'reward' purposeful stupidity. As citizens of Jerusalem, the

Arabs not only had the right to vote in municipal elections, they were also eligible to receive social security and welfare benefits from Israel. Thus, by 2012, the impoverished annexed Arab citizens of East Jerusalem were receiving upwards of one billion shekels (some 300 million dollars) a year in various entitlement payments from the Israeli government. This was more or less equivalent to the amount of money American Jewry transferred to Israel by way of the *United Israel Appeal*. In other words, since money is fungible, American Jewry was indirectly financing the social services of people inclined to support the destruction of the Jewish state and who, in any case, did not want to be part of it.

American-Jewish businessman Irving Moskowitz was one example of Diaspora culpability in a disastrous course of behavior that eventually lost all of Jerusalem to the Jewish people. Moskowitz had established a foundation that financed Jewish housing projects in Arab neighborhoods. The foundation used the law to reclaim Jewish property abandoned during Israel's 1948 War of Independence; the Palestinians had no equivalent legal right to reclaim their abandoned property. Israel's enemies used such examples to justify calling Israel an Apartheid state – inequality before the law forming the basis for daily life in Israel. This naïve and wrongheaded American Jewish behavior, in aggregate, contributed to the weakening of Israeli society, of Israel-Diaspora relations and thus to the eventual downfall of the Jewish State as well as their own communities.

Chapter Fifteen

With friends like these who needs enemies?

The evolution of Christian and right-wing political attitudes towards Israel and the Jews changed the very character of mainline American Jewish organizations to a degree that their policies and general attitudes eventually alienated substantial segments of young American Jewry. It also functioned as a tailwind for the misconceived policies of various Israeli governments – particularly concerning settlements in the occupied territories.

The Evangelical Embrace

Yitzhak Rabin's greatest tactical and strategic success as Israel's ambassador to the United States after the 6-Day-War was to establish the foundations for modern Evangelical

Christian support for Israel. This tactical and strategic success evolved over the years into a grand-strategic misfortune. It impacted negatively on Israeli policy and subsequent American Jewish identification with Israel. Rabin had perceived the eroding support for Israel amongst liberals and progressives following the 6-Day War, as well as the political awakening of the previously politically quiescent evangelical community. This was a community whose grassroots had long identified with classic American populism, which along with many American conservatives had heretofore been rather anti-Semitic. They often accepted the classic stereotypes of Jewish bankers exploiting salt of the earth 'regular folks'. Yet, the theology of *The Second Coming* facilitated a resurgence of Christian Zionism amongst the evangelical masses that was of great short-term strategic benefit to Israel, but foretold a grand strategic catastrophe.

As described above, various Bible-reading Protestant denominations and individuals had a long history of advocating for the rebirth of a Jewish State for their own theological reasons. The Christian Zionism that was amenable to Rabin's initiative was called *Premillennial Dispensationalism* and originated in the 19th century. It posited a central role for a revived Jewish state in 'the end of days'. They believed that Jesus would return to Earth when all the Jews in the world returned to their biblical homeland, *the entire Land of Israel*, and accepted Jesus as their savior. The crushing victory of Israel in the 6-Day War animated this theological segment of Evangelical thinking. Since the Jews had won against all odds, their victory was evidently the hand of God setting the stage for the 'end times': the Jews would return to Israel and there accept Jesus as their savior and then Jesus would come again. The Jews had been transformed from 'blood suckers' to 'vehicles of redemption.'

This Evangelical worldview served the strategic needs of mystical right-wing Jewish settlers whose own religious worldview envisioned the nations of the world as the servants of Israel. Many Israelis (especially the most radical religious settlers) agreed with Rabbi Ovadia Yosef who stated that: "The sole purpose of non-Jews is to serve Jews". He said that Gentiles served a divine purpose: "Why are Gentiles needed? They will work, they will plow, they will reap. We will sit like an effendi and eat. That is why Gentiles were created". In the eyes of many Orthodox settlers Evangelicals filled the role of the servant Gentile.

Both groups (settlers and Evangelicals) had adherents that felt that Rabin was assassinated as divine punishment for Oslo and that Sharon fell into a coma as divine punishment for withdrawing from Gaza. Given this, the Evangelicals were inclined towards a view favorable to the most extreme and mystical faction of the settler movement, and eventually became an American subdivision of settler propaganda. They were hostile to all concepts of territorial compromise and, as a significant faction of the Republican Party, became active subverters of American initiatives for a Middle East peace based on territorial compromise. As Donald E. Wagner, professor and director of the *Center for Middle Eastern Studies* at the University in Chicago, put it: "Christian Zionists insist that all of historic Palestine – including all the land west of the Jordan which was occupied by Israel after the 1967 war – must be under the control of the Jewish people, for they see that as one of the necessary stages prior to the Second Coming of Jesus." [73]

Mainstream Jewish organizations initially had grave reservations about Rabin's outreach to the Evangelicals because they were alien to the cultural and socio-economic character of the Jewish community. But the Evangelical embrace corresponded to the gradual drift of liberal mainstream Protestant denominations away from dialogue with the Jewish community into open hostility to Israel. Various Presbyterian, Lutheran, Methodist, Quaker and other Protestant organizations as well as the National Council of Churches actually petitioned Congress to end military assistance to Israel. Some attributed this activist enmity towards Israel to declining church attendance stimulating a desire for 'relevance' by way of fashionable progressive social activism. This politically correct 'relevance' had exactly the opposite affect these 'Christians' purportedly desired: it exacerbated the historical resentment Jews had against mainstream Christianity and by doing so, actually strengthened the Israeli right-wing.

Rise of the Neo-Cons

A corresponding development away from Judophobia had been developing in conservative American politics. In the 1950s and 1960s, the conservative intellectual William Buckley had successfully marginalized the anti-Semites within the conservative movement. This removed a major psychological barrier for solidly liberal Jewry to reconsider their political affiliation and move over into the conservative camp, other things being equal. Especially since the post 6-Day War political left had become less supportive of and even hostile to Israel. In the 1970s, the Democratic Party had become increasingly dominated by the radical dovishness of George McGovern and the post-Vietnam, post-Watergate, post blue-collar generation. As a result, many mainstream "FDR Jewish Democrats" no longer felt at home in the Democratic Party.

When Ronald Reagan (some of whose best Hollywood friends really were Jews) was elected President (with the highest percentage of Jewish votes of any Republican candidate since Eisenhower), the stage was set for the emergence of the neo-cons, many of whom had been liberal Jewish intellectuals in the FDR tradition but who had become disgusted with the trajectory of the McGovernite Democratic Party. Following the fall of the Soviet Union and the creation of the single super-power global reality, predominately Jewish neo-cons formulated a new political ideology which might be described either as an American version of the Roman peace or a right-wing iteration of Trotsky's worldwide revolution: the United States dominating the world for the 'benefit' of the world – an American iteration of Messianism. This ideology was to be realized by a policy of robust, uncompromising and unapologetic military power. This was a frame of mind that had been influenced by the military successes of Israel. To a large extent, Jewish neo-con entry into WASP and 'redneck' Republicanism was dependent on their own Jewish manliness having been redefined by the military history of macho Israel. Many Diaspora Jewish men felt their own manhood had been redeemed by Israel's success in the 6-Day War; thus predisposing them to the more hawkish elements of Israel. In regard to Israel, the neo-cons quickly made common cause with the Evangelicals and other fundamentalist Christian Zionists.

As a consequence the Republican Party came to identify support for Israel with support for the Likud and anything right of the Likud. If a Democratic politician voiced views about the Middle East similar to those of Israel's Center/ Left parties or criticized Israeli policy in ways that were even less critical than what patriotic Center/Left Israelis were saying, they were immediately attacked as being anti-Israel. This desiccated level of discourse impacted on many mainstream Jewish organizations. American Jewish critics of Israel's policy were marginalized and since many of them were secular, they were increasingly alienated from Jewish identity as such because of racist comments and writings by many Israeli Rabbis. AIPAC and other mainstream Jewish organizations had become a de facto branch of the Likud, to an extent that led Rabin and Peres at various times to threaten breaking off contact. As one Israeli journalist put it:

> ... despite its protestations ... AIPAC has historically operated more comfortably with right wing governments and with their "whole world is against us philosophy", to the point that in the 80's and 90's it was accused of promoting the right's agenda even when the leftist governments of Shimon Peres and Yitzhak Rabin were in power.[74]

In aggregate, this coalition led to the mindless support by the organized Jewish community of a "unified" Jerusalem and pro-Israel public opinion. The subsequent catastrophe the Jerusalem issue caused the Zionist project is now a matter of historical record.

The 2012 Presidential elections were the turning point for the Likud-linked Jewish lobby. This election clearly indicated a growing alienation of many American Jews from the neo-con 'party-line' of Jewish communal life. Despite frenzied opposition to President Obama on the Jewish blogosphere by Jewish Republicans and Orthodox Jews over a period of 4 years and the implicit (if not explicit) support for Romney by most Jewish organizations and the Israeli government, 69% of American Jewry still voted for Obama. Israel clearly was no longer the number one priority for the majority of non-Orthodox American Jews. There was growing resentment against Israel's discriminatory policies towards non-Orthodox Jews. There was also tremendous antipathy towards the crudities of a 'modern' Republican Party, completely identified with the Israeli government (especially the Tea Party, birthers, voter suppression, and advocacy for government interference in women's reproductive rights) The destruction of Israel could, to a large degree, be attributable to the criminal negligence of American Jewish organizations that had sided with the most reactionary elements in American society in order to support the most hawkish Israeli governments in history.

Chapter Sixteen

The Poverty of Israeli Public Relations

Rational *Hasbara* (PR) is always dependent on rational policy and cannot be based on resentment. Resentment can provide energy, but it must never be the driver of public relations either in substance or in tone. By trying to explain the unexplainable and to sell the unsellable, Israeli *Hasbara* missed myriad opportunities to strengthen Israel's grand strategic position. In order to feel better about its failures and justify itself, Israeli *Hasbara* focused almost exclusively on Jewish and philo-Jewish media consumers. It was a classic case of preaching to the converted. Huge amounts were invested in Google ads, email chain letters and articles, specialty magazines, blogs, and exposé books. The 'gurus' of Israeli *Hasbara* would brag about these intense activities. Right-wing activists were sent on lecture tours to preach to the converted. They would brag that they were successful in selling the settler position on the territories and that it was only a weakness of will and Zionist fervor that prevented the world from loving us and understanding the justice of 'our' cause ('our' meaning anything right of the Likud).

How to effectively engage non-Jewish and non philo-Jewish media and public opinion had never been dealt with very successfully, even by left-wing governments. The psychology of this was understandable – why set yourself up for failure when you could guarantee success. So huge sums and great efforts were spent on convincing the already convinced – a group that due to inexorable demographics was shrinking gradually year by year. The failures were dismissed by the Israeli Right as being due to the inherent anti-Semitism of the world; a claim that reflected a certain degree of truth, but like all such claims was overly simplistic and self-justifying and did nothing to get to the bottom of the problem, which was that rational *Hasbara* depended fundamentally on rational policy. A rational Jewish *Hasbara* campaigns based on rational policy would have had two aspects: negative and positive. Negative *Hasbara* would be aimed at *de-legitimizing* Arab/Muslim and certain NGO and media positions vis-à-vis Israel, Zionism and the Jews. Positive *Hasbara* would have been based on Israel's achievements.

All effective *Hasbara* is a variant of the strategy of the indirect approach, and must be based on one's concrete achievements and value for society (in the case of positive *Hasbara*) and on the real and self-evident flaws of one's enemy (in the case of negative *Hasbara*). It must never contradict facts and truth, must always expose the selective facts of the enemy and always strive for context. Let us examine some ideas proposed at the time but never adopted by those in power.

The Jewish Energy Project

How would a strategy of allying with environmental and alternative energy groups to weaken oil power have paid *Hasbara* dividends? Dr. Chaim Weizmann, world renowned organic chemist and first president of Israel, called for weakening oil power even before the creation of the state. In Chapter 43 of his autobiography *Trial and Error* entitled "Science and Zionism", which he had written several months *before* the establishment of the State, he observed that:

> The question of oil ... which hovers over the Zionist problem, as it does, indeed, over the entire world problem, is a scientific one ... it had always been my view that Palestine (the future state of Israel) could be made a center of the new scientific development which would get the world past the conflict(s) arising from the monopolistic position of oil.[75]

He went on to describe in detail how it might be done and how this would have created three major industries in Africa. He based his plan on the *acetone-butanol fermentation process*; a pioneering procedure in the development of biotechnology that he had developed. This was an anaerobic process that produced acetone, n-butanol and ethanol out of starchy plants that could have easily been grown in African climates. It enabled Great Britain to mass produce acetone for its war industry during WWI. Acetone was an essential ingredient of cordite that prior to the war Great Britain had to import. Weizmann subsequently leveraged this scientific achievement in the service of the British war effort into the political achievement of the Balfour Declaration.

Imagine the PR potential of this undertaking. How the Zionist project would have been inherently tied not only to solving the energy/environment conundrum but also to the substantive development of one of the poorest places on earth. Now let us imagine if Israel had proactively turned itself into a global hub of alternative energy research – using the Internet as the means to crowd research and develop different ideas from all over the world. Israel would have become a symbol of enlightenment. The environment/energy conundrum being the central issue of human civilization in the first decades of the 21st century, Israel would have been seen to be on the side of the angels. This would have been the kind of PR 'marketing' that would have sold itself without any need for slick 'explainers'.

Additionally, less Persian Gulf oil money would have been contributed to universities and dozens of spurious *Middle*

East Studies Programs dedicated to producing anti-Israel partisans rather than objective scholars. Less oil money would have also limited the dissemination of anti-Semitic and anti-Israel literature. The oil states' influence over the international investment community and media would have lessened. The relative power of international oil companies, which historically had been grand strategic partners of Arab PR and lobbying, would have rapidly declined, just as the relative power of international high tech companies with a significant Israeli presence continued to grow. Israel's own knowledge-intensive developments in information technology, alternative energy, materials science, medical technology, bio-tech and nanotech would have continued to be a backbone of positive *Hasbara*.

Debunking Aid Dependence

Another substantive step would have been to announce that Israel no longer needed American aid. This would have been a *Hasbara* coup of the first order because it would have enabled Israel to demonstrate the nature of American aid and compare it to the direct and indirect aid provided to the Arabs – especially the aid the USA was providing to the oil-rich Gulf states. This would have been especially important because of the extreme misinformation about the extent of American aid to Israel as well as the Arab and anti-Israel delusion that America could have pressured Israel by withholding aid. Professors Stephen Walt and John Mearsheimer in *The Israel Lobby and U.S. Foreign Policy* [76] beat this issue to death as one 'demonstration' of how the Jews dominated American policy-making to the detriment of America's vital interests. They saw this aid as especially wicked, given Israel's high standard of living.

The very act of declaring "we no longer need this aid" would not only have been a *Hasbara* coup in its own right, but would also have given Israel and American Jewry the opportunity to set the record straight regarding the nature of American aid. By 2012, *all* American aid to Israel was military, with over 80% given as credits to buy materiel from America's military industries. The Israeli Ministry of Defense maintained a delegation of about 400 buyers in the United States to take advantage of this. This above-mentioned fact, that part of the aid indirectly subsidized American industry and involved some 40,000 American jobs could have been widely advertised when forgoing the aid. The remaining 'discretionary' aid was dedicated to R&D conducted in Israel, but in great part also served the interests of the American military. Indeed, many Israeli enhancements of American military systems were shared freely with the Pentagon. While in the short-term this arrangement seemed good for Israel, in the long-term, the grand strategic damage to Israel in accepting this aid outweighed any economic or military benefit.

Could Israel have afforded the luxury of forgoing the aid? It might have had to spend a billion or so out of its own budget to buy systems absolutely vital to its security, but given

Israel's mature economy this would not have constituted an outrageous burden. In 2014 Israel's GDP was approaching $300 billion and its budget was $113 billion. Israel was receiving about $3 billion in aid yearly or about 1% of Israel's GDP and less than 3% of its budget. Forgoing this would have been a burden, but not an unbearable one. Israel might have had to temporarily increase its debt-to-GDP ratio, which in 2013 stood at 70% (compared to America's which was over a 100% and Singapore's which was 111%). As Israel's economy and budget was growing on average 3- 4% a year as opposed to a 2% population growth, it would have taken only about one year of economic growth to make up for the loss of American aid.

The PR advantages of this course of action would have been enormous. It would have enabled Israel to compare the indirect aid that the United States provided to the oil rich Arab Gulf States with its own. The US military had spent about $50 billion a year policing the Persian Gulf since the First Gulf War in 1991 in order to guarantee the security and survival of the Arab Gulf States. This was *independent* of the expense of the second war in Iraq. In other words, by 2013 the United States had, in effect, given over one trillion dollars in military aid to Kuwait, Saudi Arabia, The United Arab Emirates, Qatar and Bahrain. Since this was embedded *within* the American military budget it was not perceived as aid. Declaring it no longer needed aid would have been an opportune time for Israel's new *Hasbara* campaign to point this out to American and world opinion.

In conjunction with the Jewish Energy Project, this would also have been an opportune time for the organized Jewish community and its allies in the non-Jewish community to advocate for a serious effort to wean the United States off of oil. The actual cost to the American economy (when internalizing these and other costs) of gas at the pump was over $10 a gallon in 2013. Half of America's trade deficit at the time was from importing oil; greater than imports from China. This represented over one million lost American jobs.

Walt and Mearsheimer's book had dwelt on the fact that by 2010 the United States had provided Israel with about 140 billion dollars in aid over its first 60 years; it was actually $233.7 billion adjusted for inflation by 2013. This was a reasonable estimate. European critics often referred to this aid to demonstrate that Israel could not have existed except as an economic colony of the United States thus implying the illegitimacy of the very existence of Israel. Israeli and Jewish PR never responded to these kinds of arguments in a convincing way – usually using vague references to "shared values", "special relationship" and deep "mutual admiration". They could have pointed out that Europe itself could not have existed without the economic and military power of the United States. Lend Lease in WWII had cost the United States 650 billion dollars in inflation adjusted money (400 billion to Great Britain alone and another 200 billion to the Soviet Union). The Marshall Plan had cost 5.4% of American GDP in the years 1948-1952, which would have been equivalent to over $800 billion in 2014. Add to this the cost of the US NATO mission in Europe and its indirect contribution to Europe's economic recovery and United States aid to Europe in the 65 years between 1935 and 2000 totaled close to two trillion dollars. More importantly, consider what Israel did with the $240 billion in aid it received in the 65 years between 1948 and 2013. It absorbed millions of destitute immigrants and built a vigorous economy while having to maintain a heavy defense burden. Compared to the aid the EU had given to Ireland and Greece by 2012, this was really insignificant.

Ireland had received about $60 billion from the EU between 1973 (when it joined the Union) and 2008. It received another $112 billion in 2010 to bail out its banks and an additional $50 billion in 2011 to stimulate its construction industry. This was a total of $222 billion over 40 years for a country of 4.5 million with no existential security threats and almost no defense budget or destitute immigration. It was more aid than Israel received from the United States, German reparations and Jewish contributions combined from 1973 to 2012. What Greece eventually cost the EU is anybody's guess. In 2012 European Commission boss Jose Manuel Barroso estimated that the eventual total EU cost of aid to Greece following the economic crises would be about 500 billion dollars. Highlighting these facts would have gone a long way to deflecting mendacious European criticism of US support of Israel, as well as disabusing the Arab and Muslim delusion that Israel would have disappeared without American aid.

Chapter Seventeen

The Poverty of Israeli Politics

Proper Use of the 'Peace Process'

Peace with the Palestinians would have been the ultimate positive *Hasbara*. Unfortunately, by the first decade of the 21st century this had turned out not to be a realistic ambition. The Palestinians had turned down Ehud Barak's initiative in 2000 – 95% of the territories plus East Jerusalem as the capital (a proposal supported at the time by over 60% of Israel's Jewish population) – as well as Ehud Olmert's offer in 2005, which was even more generous (and also included East Jerusalem). In hindsight, the claim of the Israeli Left that the settlement project was an existential danger to the Zionist project proved to be correct; it ultimately bore great responsibility for the demise of Israel. Yet it is also clear, as the Israeli Right claimed, that the settlements were not the immediate issue in regards to peace. If the Palestinians had accepted Barak's offer in 2000 there would have been half the settlers there were in 2013. And when Prime Minister Netanyahu suspended settlement activity for 10 months in 2012-13, this did not bring the Palestinians to the table. The issue always was Israel's existence, not settlements – which we now know was a convenient Palestinian excuse.

But justifiable skepticism about a final, comprehensive peace notwithstanding, a robust involvement in 'the peace process' would have done wonders for Israel's public relations. Neither the Left nor the Right differentiated between peace and peace process; a lack of intellectual subtlety[77] that proved disastrous. Israel began to convey the impression that it was the obstructionist. Participating in discussions with the Palestinians – as well as cooperating with them on a myriad of issues (which was the on-the-ground reality) – would have been beneficial to Israel by reducing both security tension and external pressure. That they did not pursue this line of action – i.e. saying no to every initiative in order to placate domestic public opinion of the Israeli Right – contributed greatly to turning Israel into a pariah state.

Bankruptcy of the Israeli Left

Basically the Israeli Left's "post-Zionist" course of action and tone of voice was unintelligent and in the eyes of many Israelis, immoral. Following the 6-Day War they increasingly began dealing with "The Palestinian Problem" – what was "good" and "just" vis-à-vis the Palestinians, rather than what was good for the Jews – as had classic Ben Gurionist Labor Zionism. This not only alienated the healthy instincts of Jews who were not ashamed to relate to events as Zionist Jews (the vast majority of the populace) but led the Left into practical and moral inconsistencies which required complex philosophical justification arguments of little polemical value and questionable veracity. The Israeli (and international) Left blamed the occupation for overt Palestinian contempt for Jewish aspirations; for Palestinian treatment of gays and women; for international media bias as well as the massive corruption in the Palestinian Authority. Cutting themselves off from the "common" man and adapting an irritatingly condescending attitude of smug self-righteousness neutralized the effect of even their most rational arguments against the occupation and the settlement project.

Their most egregious offense was on the question of the refugees. Rather than precisely defining the problem according to international law and acknowledging the illegal double standard of the UN, they disparaged initiatives to give voice to the Jewish refugees from Muslim countries as being an obstacle to peace. This of course automatically alienated 50% of the Jewish population – many of whom had suffered the most because of the economic consequences of the settlement project and were thus potentially more open to the arguments of the Left, if the Left had not alienated them with their supercilious rhetoric.

The Left wanted to be "right" rather than effective – they had become the living caricature of Bobby Kennedy's bon mot that "the Left is never happier than when they are going down to defeat together in a just cause". The condescending sigh of despair at the ignorance of a public infected with false consciousness became the hallmark of the Left, rather than arguments that related specifically to the interests of the Jewish population. Rather than constantly drumbeating the wasted budgets in the territories and the long-term security threats to the Zionist state because of the occupation, they complained endlessly about the suffering of the poor Palestinians, refusing to criticize them for the 2000 Camp David debacle, or their persistent unintelligent decisions in general. They became 'reverse' racists, articulating a "soft racism of low expectations" which in the extreme became a "hard racism of no expectations". If they had argued what is good for the Jews, and understood that what is good for the Jews changes from period to period, they could have justified the occupation of Arab towns and villages during the 1948 War of Independence while making the point it had become disastrous for Jewish interests by 2000 – that context is everything. When you stick to this method of arguing you are consistent (why OK then and bad now) and you use a methodology that is accessible to the reasoning powers of the average individual.

The self-righteous moralistic method leads one into constant offences against agreed-upon national symbols which, even when your points are proven to be correct, only alienates the public from you even more. The Left would have been wise to have taken the advice of Benjamin Franklin, who pointed out that you never really win an argument you only make an enemy. Patriotism and religion are the common man's access to a kind of transcendent sublimity; you offend these at your own risk. An example is the American Left burning the flag during Vietnam which led to the Reagan era. The Israeli Left, visiting Arab villages and flashing 'V' for victory signs *against* the army, was seen by large portions of the Israeli general public as identifying with the enemy. Many Israelis felt that most Arabs would have slit their throats if they had the chance. Rational policy cannot be based on sympathy for or empathy with the perceived enemy – no matter how downtrodden that enemy is.

The claim to moral symmetry of much of the Left (we are as bad as they are, if not worse) was totally false and did to the Israeli Left what it did to the American Left when they drew this symmetry between the Soviets (Stalin) and McCarthyism. As politically incorrect as it might have been, it had to be said that the societal indifference to brutality on the Arab side was much greater than on the Israeli side. As Arthur Koestler once put it in a different context:

> ... to those who hold that there is nothing to choose between Western imperialism and Eastern totalitarianism ... such false equations are mostly drawn by people who have no experience of either the one or the another, and are

consequently unable to appreciate the difference in degree
... a difference which may sound somewhat abstract to
radical idealists, but not to the people directly concerned.
To live under a regime whose inherent structure imposes
a limit on its possibilities of doing evil, or under a regime
which has no limits, is a difference which comprises the
essence of human progress ... The democracies in their
present form may be cold comfort, but they are comfort
nevertheless. They are the unheated shelters where men,
shivering, can still huddle together in the totalitarian
blizzard.[78]

Israel's constitutionalist democracy and Jewish history were
inherent structures that imposed limits on the possibilities
of doing evil. Arab/Muslim society had no such inherent
structures – indeed its inherent historical narratives often
validated indifference to such limits. This, of course, did not
excuse the political stupidity of the Jews. The bankruptcy of
Israeli politics (Right and Left) caused Zionism to deal with
the Palestinian problem more than with the Jewish problem.
When all your intellectual capital is invested in your enemy
rather than yourself, you eventually commit national suicide.

Bankruptcy of the Settlement Project

The settlements in the territories were not immoral, they were
not illegal, and they were not the primary obstacles to peace.
The issue was never legal, moral or historical; the issue was
always political and politics is fundamentally a question of

smart or *stupid*. The argument for or against the settlements in the occupied territories should have been made on the basis of whether they were *smart* or *stupid* in regards to what was good for the Jews; whether the settlements contributed to the flourishing of the Jewish people in the 21ˢᵗ century.

Some of the post Six-Day War suburbs of Jerusalem and the middle class settlements contiguous to Israel's pre-Six-Day War borders did contribute to Israel's vital interests. The isolated ideological settlements, on the other hand, proved to be a tremendous burden on and a detriment to all grand strategic aspects of Israeli policy. They were an economic and social drag. The vast funds poured into them could have been better used for expanding educational services and building infrastructure in Israel proper. They did not contribute to Israel's security but rather were a tremendous burden on the Israeli army, consuming security resources that could have been better used elsewhere. The vast number of man-hours spent guarding settlements undermined the army's training regime, damaging its preparedness. A more subtle process was the damaging of the human quality of the officer corps. People good at occupation are not necessarily good in actual warfare. Also, the settlements presented the army with a border that was in effect over 1,500 kilometers long, over four times the length of the border before the Six-Day War. Simple security calculus should have dictated the following: ever-diminishing concentrations of military assets on ever- lengthening lines of defense equals less security, while ever thickening concentrations of military assets on ever shorter lines of defense equals more security.

The settlements certainly did not contribute politically. Almost every embarrassing political difficulty Israel experienced since the Six-Day War was because of ideological settlements or their supporters, and not a single country in the world changed its mind regarding the official, legally constituted borders of the State of Israel because of them. The settlements also eroded the moral self-confidence of large segments of Israeli society. For many Israelis the settlements were a cause of alienation that tarnished the label of Zionism, and weakened the spiritual fortitude and moral certainty of Israel at large. Many Israelis abhorred the settlements and resented doing reserve duty because of them. One of the causes for the increased shirking of reserve duty was the unwillingness of many otherwise good and patriotic Israelis to guard the settlements. More important was identifying Zionism with the settlements and calling opponents of the settlement project post-Zionists and even anti-Zionists. By doing this the settlers and their supporters contributed to the spread of a nihilistic post-Zionism that increasingly infected Israeli society. The erosion of Zionist moral self-confidence on the part of large segments of the Israeli public was to a considerable extent attributable to the misguided Settlement Project.

The question was never whether the settlers were brave or idealistic but whether the Settlement Project was smart or stupid, whether it contributed to or detracted from the values, goals and aims of Zionism as it tried to redefine itself in the 21ˢᵗ century. The British Light Brigade was composed of men who were brave and idealistic beyond measure but their famous charge was an example of colossal stupidity. General Lee's Confederate soldiers were brave and idealistic beyond measure, but Pickett's charge at Gettysburg was not smart and the cause it represented was not sublime. Israel's settlement policy could have been compared to the ill-fated British landing at Gallipoli in World War I, upon which the German Admiral De Robeck commented "Gallant fellows, these soldiers; they always go for the thickest place in the fence." Israel's settlement policy compelled Israeli diplomacy to always try to break through the thickest part of the diplomatic fence, the one and perhaps only place where Arab political superiority was manifest.

In political life stupidity is the greatest sin, not immorality or illegality. It is stupidity that does the greatest harm to human endeavor. If we were to judge what was pro-Zionist and what was anti-Zionist according to contribution to or deleterious effect on the economy, security, society, overall morale and moral fortitude of Israel, we would have concluded that the ideological settlements in the occupied territories constituted the most anti-Zionist activity conducted by any group of Jews since the advent of the Zionist project itself. Rational policy would have declared that the Jews had an *absolute right* to all the occupied territories but also the *absolute right*

not to exercise that right if exercising it would cause serious damage to other vital rights and needs.

Chapter Eighteen

The Bankruptcy of Labor Zionism

Labor Zionism's failure to reinvent itself after establishing the state laid the groundwork for the rise of a Likud paradigm. Instead of dealing in an imaginative way with the new reality they themselves had created, they demonstratively resented what they saw as the 'masses' turning their backs on them "after all we have done for them..."

Labor Zionism celebrated the Jewish return to agricultural activity and the creation of an industrial Jewish proletariat – the muscular Jew. They called this the "normalization" of the Jewish People, and perceived it as having inherent ideological value. But by the advent of the 21st century it was clear that both agricultural and industrial work were periodic values at best. The Labor Zionist establishment celebrated agricultural and conventional labor-intensive industrial activities way beyond the periods they were relevant for, to the detriment of the ongoing health of Israel's economy, society and environment, as well as its own political standing. Because agriculture was celebrated as a primary value, and even as a metaphor for the return of the Jews to their ancient homeland, policy makers were loath to take a hard and rational look at what agriculture really entailed in the 21st century. In 2014 Israel was the 14th driest country in the world in terms of available water per capita. Oman, Algeria, Tunisia, Egypt, Morocco and Syria all had more water per capita than Israel – Egypt four times more and Syria eight times more. Moreover, the Jews had no wish to work in a sector with such an abysmal pay scale. Water-poor Israel subsidized the export of water (for that is what you are exporting when you export agricultural products) to water-rich Germany, France and Scandinavia in order to create jobs for Thai guest workers. And yet "Jewish" agriculture remained a Zionist ideal!

The justifications for labor-intensive industries were no less irrational and their consequences for Israel's economy and society no less detrimental. From the early 1970s, these industries survived only because of massive direct and *indirect* subsidies. But even with subsidies, pay scales in labor-intensive industries seldom exceeded minimum wage, even for people with years of seniority. These industries formed the economic base of the Development Towns and thus became a major contributor to the ongoing deepening of the social/ethnic gap and alienation from Labor intellectuals who sang the praises of physical work from their air conditioned offices. One cannot have minimum wage industries and close social gaps; in a dynamic society such as Israel's, the gap could only widen as long as such industries existed. So, even massive direct and indirect subsidies could not sustain Israel's labor-intensive industries, which as with other developed countries, eventually moved to the developing world.

In contrast, the unemployment figures in the non-industrial, non-pioneering, non-proletariat Sharon area (Kfar Saba, Ra'anana, Hod Ha'Sharon, Herzliya) just north of Tel Aviv were less than 3%, and this area was a hotbed of hi-tech, sophisticated services and innovation which contributed billions of dollars a year to Israel's export figures. According to classic Labor Zionist ideology, this area had nowhere near the Zionist value that settlements or Development Towns or near bankrupt kibbutzim had. According to classic Labor ideology, the residents of these towns were, by definition, self-absorbed, egoistic, bourgeois, hedonistic yuppies alienated from "authentic" expressions of Zionism. That these areas produced a disproportionate number of citizens that served in the elite units of the Army as well as a disproportionate amount of the economic and professional value and tax revenues that enabled the Zionist enterprise to exist at all, was conveniently ignored. Ironically they also produced the largest number of Labor voters. Thus, the Israeli political paradox was created – the "bourgeoisie" voted Labor and the Jewish laborers from working class neighborhoods and development towns voted Likud.

The crisis of labor-intensive industries could have been avoided. By the late 1970's it was clear to anyone who cared to analyze the trends that labor-intensive industries had no future in the developed world. Intelligent policy makers in other developed countries such as Japan began to shed their labor-intensive industries gradually, moving them to cheap labor developing countries. They combined this economic policy with a major redirection of the educational system. The gradualness of the process – shedding older workers as they achieved retirement age while not absorbing younger workers – enabled the radical shrinking of the work force of these sectors *without social dislocation*. Young people entering the work force were directed to other lines of work while younger workers were retrained for other branches of the economy.

Labor policy makers, on the other hand, still infatuated with the ideological myth of the Jewish industrial worker and having no alternative answers for the Development Towns, were incapable of changing course. They were also under pressure from Labor leaders (in the Histadrut), more concerned with their own political power as heads of large unions than with the long term welfare of their members. As Upton Sinclair once put it, "it is hard to make someone understand something when his salary depends on not understanding it". The resultant social dislocation and trauma bear witness to the shortsighted foolishness of perpetuating this periodic Labor Zionist "value" long after its historical shelf-life had expired. Here the contradictions of the Zionist Left were laid bare, the contradiction between Zionist ideologies that celebrated the Jew returning to physical labor and a Socialist ideology of a decent living wage. These two ideologies could never cohabit in a hi-tech, globalized world.

Peace, Peace Process and Peace Agreements

Following the Oslo agreements the Israeli Left developed an infatuation with the instruments of past success at the expense of updated grand strategic focus and intellectual clarity vis-à-vis the peace process. Israel's peace activists consistently confused the primary value of peace with the secondary or periodic value of a manageable Cold War reached by way of peace agreements. For them, Israel should have been in continuous negotiations with the Palestinians and the Syrians in order to achieve a peace agreement. The historical success of this particular formula vis-à-vis the Egyptians and the Jordanians was not in dispute. Indeed the success was so profound in its implications that many Israelis became infatuated with the *formula* at the expense of possible alternative interim aims.

This is understandable. Since its foundation, Israel's primary grand strategic aim was to neutralize hostility towards the Jewish State in order to gain breathing room to develop and absorb as many immigrants as possible. This aim was achieved with Egypt and Jordan by way of a peace agreement; it was achieved, de-facto, for seven years with the Palestinians by way of the Oslo Accords; it was achieved, de facto, with Syria across the Syrian border by way of Israel's military might. It was not achieved with Syria's proxy state, Lebanon, or its proxy organizations Hezbollah and Jihad, and hence not finally with Syria. The Second Intifada prevented it from being fully achieved with the Palestinians.

Israel's aim should have been peace and quiet in order to develop. If peace agreements provided peace and quiet, as in the case of Egypt and Jordan, so much the better. If the unrestrained quest for a peace agreement generated an Intifada, so much the worse. Contrary to accepted wisdom at the time, Israel had not achieved its primary aim of real peace with either Egypt or Jordan. What it had achieved was a manageable Cold War, a great achievement in and of itself. The Egyptians had been telling Israelis for years that "we recognize you but we don't accept you". Yet the Israeli Left's fixated infatuation with peace caused it to live in an illusion that often endangered the peace process itself. For example, when Shimon Peres coined the phrase "New Middle East" Israelis greeted it with bemused impatience but the Arabs greeted it with real fear and anger. They interpreted it as a catch phrase for Israeli economic colonialism of the Middle East and another example of the Jewish superiority complex expressed in paternalistic terms. Mr. Peres was sincere, but his presumption demonstrated how unrestrained naiveté and wishful thinking in regards to peace actually caused damage to the peace process.

Israel's manageable Cold War with Egypt was similar to the relationship between the United States and the Soviet Union during the Cold War. It was characterized by a combination of hesitant economic and political contacts and cooperation side by side with hostility. The hostility was unilateral, solely on the part of Egypt. There was ongoing communication, mutual political recognition, and incipient economic relations but not real peace. The determined, ongoing, focused hostility of Egypt to Israel's interests in numerous areas was similar to the American-Soviet Cold War. Egypt's Cold War with Israel was even colder than the former America-Soviet cold war, which at least maintained cultural, academic and scientific contacts. The hostility of Arab intellectuals to Israel and to the Jewish People was so pervasive that these kinds of contacts never actually occurred. If the American-Soviet Cold War was chilly, the Israel-Egyptian-Jordanian Cold War was freezing. But it still was not a shooting war and this was a tremendous Zionist achievement. Indeed, it was the greatest Zionist achievement since the establishment of the State. As Churchill had once put it "Jaw, Jaw is better than War, War".

The peace process itself was a de-facto admission on the part of the Arabs of the failure of their policy and the success of Zionist Policy. Israel achieved a great deal by way of the peace process. Egypt was removed from the ring of military threat that once surrounded Israel, thereby improving Israel's strategic position. It enabled Israel to achieve greater global political acceptability that contributed to its economic development and ability to absorb immigrants. But the relative success of the peace agreements blinded many to the essentially different reality Israel faced with the Palestinians. Barak's finalistic ambitions at Camp David may have contributed to the outbreak of the Second Intifada simply because Israel's leaders failed to realize that no matter what they proposed it would be all but impossible for the Palestinians to accept. In other words the unrestrained pursuit of the peace agreement led to armed conflict.

The Demise of Constructive Socialism

The political power of the Israeli Labor Movement had been based on the tremendous socio-economic creativity it demonstrated during the pre-state period – the era known as 'the state on the way'. This imagination was the concrete expression of Syrkin's 'Constructive Socialism' and manifested itself in the creation of the Kibbutz, Moshav, Moshav Shitufi, and Histadrut enterprises, workers' cooperatives in industry, services and transportation, as well as the creation of a relatively comprehensive health system – what Ben Gurion called 'The Workers Republic'.

All of these initiatives degenerated in the post-state era as they came to serve the political interests of the Labor party and the personal interests of Labor functionaries. Constructive Socialism was replaced by bureaucratic/politruk socialism. This generated ever-increasing resentment amongst growing numbers of citizens until Begin's Likud party dethroned Labor in 1977 in the revolt of the alienated. In the years following – in opposition or in power – Labor adopted a position which might be termed 'Social Work Socialism'. They degenerated from constructive to bureaucratic to social work socialism. The last was fundamentally composed of worn-out welfare policies adopted from Europe and America and a relentlessly repeated mantra of tired terminology and slogans. Advocating Social Democracy, calling for 'social justice' and condemning swinish Capitalism became the standard fare of their political discourse. None of this had any real operative content and was characterized more by pathos then any genuinely substantive policy proposals. By 2015 one could look back and justifiably claim that since the creation of the state, Labor had not come up with even one original social/economic idea of the kind that characterized their rule during the pre-state era.

The electoral 'surprise' of 2015 could have been partially explained by this state of affairs. When impoverished – mostly Mizrahi – voters were asked why they continued to vote Likud when Likud policies had not improved their lot, they most often replied in reference to the inertia of resentment of how they had been treated under Labor governments. But some of the more sophisticated voters simply asked rhetorically 'what does Labor (now called The Zionist Camp) policy offer that will improve my lot rather than the lot of their functionaries; what makes them any better than the Likud?' In other words, the mantra of Social Democratic slogans had no resonance with these voters, who remained unconvinced that Labor's 'social program' proposals would positively impact on them or just create more sinecures for party functionaries. In other words, nothing Labor offered could substantively erode the natural emotional identification these voters had with the Likud and the ongoing resentment towards what they felt was the condescending treatment they received from the Labor movement during the 50s and 60s.

PART IV –
THE TURNING POINT

*T*his part of the book will relate to the various turning points that signaled the decline and eventual fall of the Jewish State.

Chapter Nineteen

The PR Turning Point

Israel's public relations, or the lack thereof, had been a focal point of Jewish debate since the 1967 6-Day War. This was because there was an implicit recognition that Israel's war for survival was grand strategic and involved the entire Jewish People. Grand strategy refers to the economic, political, social and public relations resources that were available to world Jewry in addition to the military assets of Israel and perhaps most important, the moral self-confidence of Jews everywhere. Unfortunately this implicit recognition never turned into true understanding of the place of public relations as a vital part of grand strategy and not something that only explains policy. Part of the problem was that the Hebrew word for public relations – *Hasbara* – literally means explanation and not information. Explanation is to information what sales are to marketing. Nothing was more counterproductive than Israeli experts in communications appearing on television and explaining the value of their Israeli product and the essential weaknesses of the Arab competition.

The belief that smooth, well-groomed spokespeople with a high level of English could sell an Israel not backed up by an acceptable policy reinforced by a rational grand strategy was simply wrongheaded. Good products sell themselves. Rubbish does not sell no matter how good the marketing or the sales pitch. In other words, Israel could never have sold stupid policy no matter how sophisticated its PR campaign. Israel policy would have had to be reasonable to informed Western opinion in the 21st century. Trying to justify nastiness by referring to the historic nastiness of its critics was never going to work. "After America's treatment of the American Indians how can they dare criticize our so-called mistreatment of the Palestinians", or "After Europe's treatment of the Jews... etc. etc." were some typical reactions of 'patriotic' Israelis and Diaspora Jews.

Despite the utter stupidity of these kinds of self-justifications (identifying Israeli policy in peoples' minds with American atrocities against the Indians or European atrocities against the Jews, thus doing the Arabs' work for them) it was completely ineffective in trying to put critics back on their heels. Because the implicit answer of the 21st century American or European was: "Yes, we did those things; we are ashamed of them; we don't do them anymore; and if you want to be part of our club (the democratic West) you won't do them either". Given many of the concrete policies of Western countries at the time, a response like this was certainly dishonest, but political and economic power will always trump moral arguments. And since Israel's critics were bigger and more powerful, Israel really had no choice but to play the game of international *realpolitik* according to these hypocritical rules.

Historical Background

As described above, prior to the 6-Day War, Israel enjoyed a tremendous *Hasbara* advantage for both positive and negative reasons. The post-Holocaust "phoenix rising from the ashes" metaphor of a nation crushed like no other nation had ever been before taking hold of its destiny and building a progressive modern country in a barren land in the face of constant hostility against overwhelming odds excited the imagination of Europe and America, as well as large segments of the developing world. The social experiments of the Kibbutz and the Moshav as well as large-scale service and consumer cooperatives excited the imagination of the European Left and imbued Israel with a special status in the *Socialist International*. Golda Meir's standing in the *International* was comparable to that of Willy Brandt and Harold Wilson. Israel's comprehensive trade unionism (90% of the working population during its early years) gave Israel a disproportionate weight in international trade unionism when unions were much more powerful in industrialized democratic countries than they had become by the 21st

century. All this attracted the sympathies of "progressive" public opinion.

Israel's achievements also provided Diaspora Jewry with a source of pride and earned Gentile admiration. Israel was easy to sell since its concrete achievements marketed themselves. Sympathetic Jews and Gentile anti anti-Semites dominated the campuses and media. The bestselling book *Exodus* and movies such as *Exodus* and *Cast a Giant Shadow* were public relations boons that could not have been bought for billions of dollars. Moreover, the Arab competition was easy to disparage. King Saud's gold plated Cadillac and dozens of wives were objects of parody and ridicule in popular culture, from stand-up comedians to James Bond movies. Nasser and others came across as pro-Soviet dupes or thugs. The price of oil was low and dependence on Middle East oil was still marginal. Few Arab or Muslim students and fewer Muslim faculty members were on Western campuses.

But following the 6-Day War, the Arabs began to engage in marketing on a major scale. They cleverly focused on the centers of future public-opinion-making – the university campuses. This was a turning point in the Arab-Israeli conflict because it was the first and perhaps only time in their struggle with Zionism that the Arabs adopted a future-oriented strategy that would bear fruit after several decades. Zionism had been the ultimate future-oriented political movement up until the 6-Day War. Following the first Zionist Congress in Basle in 1897, Herzl had written that he had created the Jewish State, perhaps not in a year or in ten years, but certainly in 50 years. In 1947, 50 years after Herzl's futurist vision, the United Nations accepted the Partition Plan. Herzl's *The Jewish State* was a futurist essay and his novel *Old New Land* was a futurist work of fiction.

Ben Gurion was the embodiment of a Jewish Futurist (once saying that the next 1,000 years of Jewish history are more important than the last 1,000 years). His call that Israel strive to become a 'light unto the nations' was not only an expression of prophetic idealism; it was pragmatic recognition that unless Israel became a 'light unto the nations' it would not be a light unto the Jews and would not garner long-term support either from the Gentiles or the Jews. Without a transcendent future vision, the Zionist project would ultimately fail. In other words, the 'product' (the State of Israel) had to be of excellent, market-differentiated quality; it could not be a cheap imitation of Sparta or Prussia, nor could it be an ersatz Middle East version of a bourgeoisie Scandinavian welfare state. It had to be something heroic, with transcendent humanistic ambitions for the future – it had to be a "light unto the nations".

Labor Zionism, in its many manifestations, was preoccupied with creating the future Jewish utopia. As previously noted the writings of Labor Zionism's great opponent, Jabotinsky, were also characterized by a future orientation. He predicted the

demise of brute physical work as a consequence of technology
and thus of the proletariat as a historical force. His historical
writings were educational analogies intended to inspire future
action. In the third stage of the Zionist project he supported
the idea of the Jewish state becoming a laboratory to solve
the problems of the entire human race. What separated
modern religious Zionists from the ultra-Orthodox was their
affiliation with Labor Zionism and its stress on the future.
Also, as previously noted Chaim Weizmann predicted the
future negative effects of oil on world politics and Jewish
wellbeing in 1948 (before the creation of the state) and called
on the future Jewish state to make finding an alternative to oil
its primary scientific preoccupation. This future orientation
gave Israel a tremendous cultural and political advantage over
the Arabs, who had been preoccupied with past glories and
past victimizations. In the entire history of Arab Nationalism
one finds no equivalent to Herzl, Weizmann, Ben-Gurion
or Jabotinsky in terms of envisioning alternative futures for
the Arab People.

All this changed after the 6-Day War. "Practical" native-
born Israelis became a dominant force in Israeli politics.
They disdained grand visions of the future and preoccupied
themselves with the immediate. Their nickname in popular
jargon was the 'implementers' – in Hebrew the *bitzuistim*.
Moshe Dayan was the foremost exemplar of this generation.
However, following the Yom Kippur War, the spiritual
barrenness and ultimate inefficiency of a vision-free Zionism

was strongly felt and the vision vacuum was filled by *Gush Emunim* with visions of the past, not the future.

The settlement project of Gush Emunim in the occupied territories co-opted both the idealism and the instruments of the early Zionist pioneers. They claimed they were continuers of the early pioneers and the true representatives of Zionism. They replaced the Kibbutz as the face of Israel in the world. Unfortunately, many in Israel and in the West believed them. If this was 'authentic' Zionism, then perhaps Zionism itself was wrong. The seeds of post-Zionism in Israel and resurgent anti-Zionism in the West were planted. If Gush Emunim was the poster child of Zionism (and they did provide the best photo opportunities for a planet now ruled by visual media), then how could the 'explainers' sell Israel's message to a West dominated by post-colonial guilt and a developing world dominated by post-colonial resentment? Israeli policy itself began to market a negative *information* image of Israel; an image that *explanation* (Hasbara) could never really overcome.

The difference between Gush Emunim and the early pioneers was self-evident. Gush Emunim wished to reconstruct the past at the expense of the future, whilst the early pioneers had strived to use the past as an inspiration to build a better future. But the Labor and Liberal Zionist parties had become ideologically irrelevant and morally compromised by political maneuvering. They had no real response to Gush Emunim.

They had no updated future-oriented Zionist vision to offer. All they could do was fall back on past achievements no longer relevant to the postmodern reality. This facilitated the message of Gush Emunim, which acknowledged and praised past Labor achievements but portrayed itself as the natural continuation of that pioneering legacy. Labor, bragging about its past rather than offering up alternative visions of the future, just served the settler movements interests.

For Israeli public relations to really succeed there had to be a revival of future Zionist visions capable of rejuvenating Jewish idealism and Gentile admiration. Israeli public relations once again had to have a marketable product if it was to have any chance of success. As we now know, it did not develop that product and the Jewish People paid the ultimate price.

Islamification of the West

Large scale Muslim immigration to the West coincided with the decline of Israeli marketability and public relations. In 1950, Western Europe had less than a quarter of a million Muslims and two million Jews. By 2012 it had over 20 million Muslims and 1.5 million Jews. In 1950, North America had almost no Muslims. By 2001, Canada had more Muslims than Jews, while the estimated number of Muslims in the United States ranged from as little as 2 million to as many as 7 million – the larger number being the one claimed by the

Muslim community itself. By 2020, there were more Muslims than Jews in the United States and they were younger and more politically active.

These demographics alone explain a great deal regarding Israel's position in the world at the time. In fact, it is a wonder that Europe was not even more anti-Israel than it was in the first two decades of the 21st century. Israel had the revolting behavior of many of Europe's Muslims and consequent European Islamophobia to thank for this. If Muslims had been more civic-minded citizens, respectful of democratic etiquette, native Europeans would have been more inclined to side with their views on the Middle East. This is because politicians in democracies know how to count – they know how to count votes and contributions. For example, notwithstanding Harry Truman's instinctive sympathies for the nascent Jewish state, he was, after all a politician and thus countered State Department objections to recognizing Israel with "how many votes do the Arabs have?" Would he have made such a statement in the second decade of the 21st century? Would he have supported the establishment of Israel in the second decade of the 21st century – given the growing number of Muslim voters and the dependence of the democratic world on imported oil?

Following the 6-Day War, enormous numbers of Arab students, financed by oil money scholarships, poured onto Western campuses. They were well-schooled in focused, on-message propaganda slogans. Financed by their home countries, few had to work while studying. Their full time extra-curricular activity was pro-Arab and anti-Israel propaganda. It often seemed that the price of their scholarship was to become fulltime propagandists. Oil prices and Western dependence on Muslim oil increased significantly during this period, further complicating the picture. Europe was initially an easier market for Arab propagandists to penetrate than the United States. The post-colonial mindset of guilt-ridden Europeans and their loss of moral self-assurance (ironically to a large extent because of the Holocaust) made Europeans easy targets for Arab propagandists.

Unfortunately, Israel's own behavior helped the Arabs. The Israeli occupation (and the early stages of "colonial" settlements) coincided with the beginning of the special relationship with the United States, which was bogged down in Vietnam. This occurred during the height of the student revolutions of the late 1960's. The timing could not have been worse in molding the mindset of future leaders and opinion-makers in Europe and left of center political opinion in the United States. For politically correct public opinion, Israel had become a 'militaristic colonial aggressor, an ally of anti-Third World neo-imperialist America'. The Arabs, especially the Palestinians, were an oppressed and exploited Third World people. It was self-evident what position "progressive" people would take.

The special relationship Israel had enjoyed with European progressives due to the achievements of Labor Zionism began to wane. To be an academic with a "mature" view of world affairs, one had to disabuse oneself of naive support for Israel. Sentimental sympathy with previously oppressed Jews was no longer 'mature'. Now the Jews had become the oppressors. In any case, they argued, Zionism and Jewry are not one and the same. One could be an anti-Zionist without being anti-Jewish. There was no lack of Jewish intellectuals who, in order to be politically correct and transcend their own ethnic 'provinciality', gave credence to this distinction. American academia, looking over its shoulder at Europe in order to be "sophisticated", followed suit.

Jewish and Israeli students were overwhelmed by this wave of sudden hostility, while the self-confident and somewhat arrogant post 6-Day-War Israeli establishment was dismissive of the threat and provided no leadership or coherent PR strategy. Campuses and the media were seen as marginal to the centers of real power, which "manly" Israeli politicians were cultivating. Intellectuals and political commentators who were disturbed by developments were treated with condescension and disdain. Their concern for what the Gentiles were thinking was dismissed as a lingering characteristic of the ghetto Jew. There was something effeminate and 'old Jew' about this kind of worrying. Manly 'new Jews' concerned themselves with real problems and real power, not the chattering slogans of intellectual airheads. They justified their *realpolitik* indifference to these developments by misinterpreting David Ben Gurion's famous declaration: "It's not important what the goyim think (or say); it's important what the Jews do".

Paradoxically, no Israeli leader had been more concerned with what the 'goyim' thought than Ben Gurion. This was because the 'goyim' sometimes acted on what they thought, and what they did was important to the Jews. Ben Gurion never ignored or dismissed Gentile views. He always wanted to know what they were thinking. But he also knew that no matter what they thought, Israel still had the freedom to do something – something, *not anything*. Geopolitical constraints and strategies of limited aims were Ben Gurion's forte and what made him a great leader. He was for the U.N. Partition Plan and fought for it against substantial Zionist opposition because he knew it was the best deal, given the political limitations of the time. He also knew it was a window of opportunity that would close as political reality began to work against the Zionist project. He would never have uttered those infamous post 6-Day-War words "time is on our side". For him, time was never on Israel's side.

Israel's previous public relations advantage had been unplanned. It had been realized inadvertently by Israel's own achievements, by the corrupt state of the Arab world and by Hollywood. There was, therefore, no coherent, organized, 'on-message' Jewish response to the Arab propaganda machine. A hundred Arab spokesmen would use the same arguments and have the same responses to the standard journalistic questions. Fifty Jewish spokespersons would have fifty different responses.

Moreover, the occupation and the beginnings of the settlement project led Israeli political parties to splinter and reflect many shades of public opinion, from the right-wing 'annex everything' to the left-wing 'give everything back' or even having a half a dozen positions within the same party. When public opinion is so conflicted, a democracy has difficulty in formulating and executing a coherent PR campaign. What product was Israel selling: Israel the colonial power exploiting cheap Arab labor, or Israel the peace seeker and beacon of social justice? What policy was Israel 'explaining': its historic rights to the land, its territorial requirements for security, its desire for peace, its need for cheap labor, or its inability to decide what it wanted? Being the only democracy in the Middle East, it could not design or control its message when it came to the occupation. Its message was as conflicted as its internal politics. This conflicted message not only served Israel's enemies, it eventually exhausted the patience of Israel's friends and supporters. The situation this created also exhausted growing numbers of young Israelis who became alienated from the level of political discourse that resulted from this situation.

An effective *Hasbara* campaign should have begun with debunking the view that Zionism was a colonialist movement. It could have made the following points:

1. Every colonial enterprise represented or derived from an *existing* mother country or group of countries – Zionism did not.

2. No other colonial enterprise viewed itself as *returning to its homeland* – Zionism did.

3. No other *modern* colonial enterprise was driven by the desire of the colonizers to escape persecution and discrimination – Zionism was.

4. No other colonial enterprise viewed its colonial ambition as being part and parcel of their *national* cultural, psychological and moral renewal – Zionism did.

5. No other colonial enterprise satisfied itself with only *one* colony – Zionism did.

6. No other colonial enterprise desired so passionately to settle a land *devoid* of natural resources – Zionism did.

7. No other colonial enterprise desired to create an independent state (all the others saw themselves as dependent colonies of the mother country) – Zionism did.

8. No other colonial enterprise desired to create an entirely new society – Zionism did.

In other words, Zionism was unique (just like the rest of Jewish history) and thus the Middle East conflict was unique.

Unfortunately, the occupation and all of its corollaries trumped any rational argument that Israel could have made.

Chapter Twenty

The Demographic
& Cultural Turning Point

We have seen the enemy and it is us! (Pogo and Israel)

In 2012, Israel's *Central Bureau of Statistics* announced that
44% of Israel's pupils would be Arab or ultra-Orthodox by
2017. The fastest rate of growth was in the country's ultra-
Orthodox (*Haredi*) schools, with an annual increase of 3.7%.
This was compared to a 2.5% annual increase in religious
Zionist schools, a 1.5% annual increase in Arab schools, and
a 1.5% annual increase at the state's secular schools (which
included immigrant children). The future economic impact
was noted in a 2013 study by the *National Economic Council*
which forecast that by 2029, the percentage of non-Haredi
Jews entering the labor force would decline from 71% to
53%. Both these predictions came about because of a lack

of political courage which had grave economic and political consequences.

The Israeli political class was afraid to publically campaign against the budgetary discrimination against the Arab population. They were equally fearful of taking on the Rabbis regarding the obscurantist educational practices of the Haredim which forbade the teaching of Science, Math, Computers and English. There were married men and women with children who had never even heard (let alone understood) words like molecule, diploma, and essay, and were still not aware that the earth rotated around the sun. Actually it would not have taken that much courage to address both issues. As one Israeli Arab economist pointed out, if the standard of living of the Israeli Arabs was equal to that of the Jews, it would raise the standard of living of the Jews by 20%. On the Haredi side there was great inherent potential to effect a revolution in attitude. Many young Haredi men and a greater number of young Haredi women were tired of living in poverty and increasingly sensitive to the non-Haredi world's view of them and greatly desired to acquire modern skills.

But long-term thinking amongst Israel's political class was limited to the next election rather than the historical needs of the Jewish people. They feared alienating the Jewish voter by advocating for Arab equality and they feared alienating the Haredi Rabbis, who played a major role in forming governmental coalitions. The so-called 'progressive' Left was just as guilty of this short-term thinking as the so-called 'racist' Right. The next election was always the alpha and omega of their intellectual imagination.

By 2017, Arab pupils comprised 26% of the overall student population; Haredi pupils, 18%; and religious Zionist pupils, 14%. In other words 44% of pupils were from cultures that were anti-Zionist or non-Zionist (Arabs and Haredim) and 58% from cultures inherently inimical to liberal constitutionalist concepts (Arabs, Haredim and Religious Zionists). When children from other households not rooted in democratic traditions were figured in (many Mizrahi and Russian-speaking immigrants) the majority of Israel's future citizens were destined to be reactionary in regard to constitutionalist attitudes. This is what was happening *within* the pre-1967 borders of Israel, and when the population of the West Bank was eventually added, the demographic picture became truly disastrous for the future of a democratic Jewish state.

Jerusalem was the key. In 2012, over 80% of elementary school children in the united Jerusalem were Arab or Haredi Jews. By 2030, close to 90% of the 'voting' citizens of the capital of the Zionist State were anti-Zionist or at best non-Zionist and 50% of Israel's voting citizens (within the pre-1967 borders) were anti-Zionist or non-Zionist with Orthodox religious Jews of all sorts comprising over 50% of the Jewish voting public nationwide. Moreover, during the first decade of the 21st century, 8,000-10,000 Jews were leaving Jerusalem every year with only 4,000-6,000 Jews moving to Jerusalem. This trend gained momentum in the subsequent decades. The demographics of this migration were instructive. The Jews leaving were on the whole young university-trained Jews with young children who increasingly could not find suitable schools in an educational system dominated by the Arab and Haredi educational systems. The Jews coming to Jerusalem were on the whole young Yeshiva students and elderly Jews from the Diaspora. It was observed that: "Jerusalem had become the elephant burial ground of the Jewish People". Its population had a large net increase despite the negative migration patterns because the Haredim had huge families subsidized directly by the state and indirectly by the municipality (not having to pay city taxes because of their poverty). So while the population increased, the municipal tax base shrank and the city turned into a huge slum – a process that had become noticeable very early on in the 21st century. By 2020, Jerusalem had earned the epithet "the Jewish Gaza".

Changing Palestinian Strategy

These statistical trends had begun to attract the attention of Palestinian intellectuals and young leaders in the first decade of the 21st century and eventually caused a major grand strategic shift in Palestinian policy. In 2012, over 250,000 East Jerusalem Palestinians had the right to vote in municipal elections under Israeli law as residents of the city. But only a minuscule number of Palestinians had exercised this right; most had refrained in protest against what they felt was the illegal annexation of East Jerusalem by Israel. This boycott had been encouraged by the Palestinian leadership to demonstrate Palestinian self-respect and sense of honor. But in the second decade of the 21st century a few Palestinian intellectuals had begun to question this policy. They described it as cutting off the Palestinian nose to spite the Israeli face.

By 2012, a cultural and sociological shift in East Jerusalemite behavior had become apparent and began to erode this policy of 'honor', to be replaced by a policy reflecting the rational interests of daily life. East Jerusalem Arabs had begun to resemble Israeli Arab citizens in their life styles and expectations – picnicking in municipal parks; favoring the Israeli matriculation exam (the *Bagrut*) over the Palestinian matriculation exam; preferring Israeli Universities over Palestinian ones, and increasingly applying for Israeli citizenship. The pitiful state of East Jerusalem's infrastructure and services was the trigger for political change that was rooted in this sociological change. Some began to speak openly about voting in order to achieve representation on the 31-seat Jerusalem city council in order to obtain better services and infrastructure for the Arab citizens of Jerusalem.

By voting en masse in the 2013 municipal election the Arabs could have obtained at least 10 seats with the Haredi parties also getting 10 seats, leaving the modern orthodox and secular Jewish parties with 11 seats between them. They did not vote in 2013, but many did in the 2018 municipal elections when they constituted 40% of the city's voters. This was precisely the percentage of votes needed to capture the mayor's seat as well as a plurality on the City Council. Yet by that time, Israel had annexed several large Jewish settlements to Jerusalem to forestall such an occurrence so that the Arabs did not gain the mayor's seat.

But the Arabs still won nine seats on the council and adopted a strategy of supporting the Haredi parties' most radical religious demands in the hopes of alienating the secular public and driving them from the expanded city. This strategy worked, and by 2030 Jerusalem had become 90% Arab and Haredi as the older neighborhoods and newly annexed suburbs emptied of modern religious and secular Israelis. The remaining 10% were the elderly and poor remnants of the mass Aliyah from Middle Eastern countries who had come to Israel in the 1950s – their children and grandchildren having left as part of the secular and modern religious exodus from the city. People with the skills to maintain a modern economy left in droves. The companies that needed such workers left with them. The capital of the Zionist State had been conquered by non-Zionists and anti-Zionists and had become an economic basket case; an economic, social and cultural desert – a failed state within a state.

The Question of Apartheid

Apartheid being an imprecise and loaded description of Israel's unique system of discrimination enabled many Israelis to hide behind a fog of self-righteous indignation and avoid confronting ugly realities. Israel was not an Apartheid state by any objective measure. Israeli Arabs were to be found in every area of Israeli life – doctors, pharmacists, dentists, lawyers, business people, and members of Knesset. They sat next to Jews on buses and in restaurants, shared the same hospital rooms, were waited on by Jewish waiters in restaurants, opened businesses and rented apartments in Jewish neighborhoods, and shopped freely in Jewish areas. They were represented in the judiciary and had representatives on the Supreme Court of Israel. In fact one of the three judges that sentenced former President Moshe Katsav to 7 years in jail for rape was an Arab. There was still significant structural discrimination and cultural prejudice against the Arabs in Israel, but it would have been difficult to term it 'Jim Crow' let alone Apartheid; it was sui generis. Thus, when critics of Israel used such terminology it aroused such indignation that it had the opposite effect and inhibited healthy self-criticism within Israeli society.

President Jimmy Carter's *Peace Not Apartheid* book was the perfect example of fashionable 'progressive' jargon and sloganeering trumping a more nuanced yet more precise critique of the stupidity of Israel's policies. The demagogic branding of Israel as an Apartheid state was simply not empirical and enabled the radical Right to maneuver the majority into fits of self-righteous indignation, thus enabling them to avoid confronting the very unique and creative system of discrimination Israel had built. That said, the situation in the occupied territories was a completely different state of affairs. By 2014, the situation in Judea and Samaria was becoming more *apartheid-like* day by day. Two separate legal systems based on ethnicity existed side by side. Two separate economic and development systems based on ethnicity existed side by side. Gross discrimination regarding allocation of water was based on ethnicity. Even a non-commissioned officer could forcibly enter a Palestinian home without probable cause or a search warrant. Jews illegally squatting on Palestinian land were not removed while the Palestinians, whose land was being squatted on, were prevented from working their land by the IDF, as they might constitute a security threat to the Jewish squatters.

Irreversibility

Every small brick of evidence boosted the theory of irreversibility that was gaining strength in the public discourse regarding the occupied territories. The theory held that it was no longer possible to seriously discuss dividing the land or evacuating the settlements, since the government's decisions, the political stalemate and the resolve of the settlers had already determined that there would be a one-state, bi-national solution. Just the nature of that state - whether it would more closely resemble a federation or Apartheid - was yet to be determined. Jerusalem embodied this irreversibility. The law of unintended consequences had prevailed. The separation barrier, along with the discrimination faced by graduates of Palestinian educational institutions, had pushed East Jerusalem youth westward. This process came on the heels of additional signs of the "Israelization" of Jerusalem's Palestinian population.

There had been a drop in fertility rates among East Jerusalem families and a rise in the participation of women in the work force. Palestinian families began moving into predominantly Jewish neighborhoods and, no less importantly, could increasingly be found in parts of West Jerusalem that had long been considered Jewish destinations, such as Sacher Park, Malcha Mall and Jaffa Street.[79] Observers of Arab society offered varying interpretations of these changes. One theory posited that Palestinian East Jerusalemites were undergoing a process of Israelization and integration similar to that which the Israeli Arabs underwent after the 1950s. Others saw this behavior as a survival tactic, a result of political apathy on the part of a young generation merely looking for a way to make it under occupation. There was also talk of the creation of a new kind of Palestinian identity that was distinct from that of Palestinians in the West Bank or the Gaza Strip, as well as from that of the Israeli Arabs.[80]

The causes were almost certainly a combination of these theories. But whatever the cause, the decade 2010-2020 witnessed greater East Jerusalemite immersion in local politics. Their lack of governmental representation had made it easier for the city, and the country as a whole, to discriminate against them when it came to apportioning the budget. By 2020, this had been neutralized. Irving Moskowitz had gotten what he and his followers had been asking for, even if not quite what they actually had in mind: a united Jerusalem, a united Land of Israel and the end of the Zionist dream. Very quickly the Arabs made common cause with the Haredim and the city hall of the capital of the Zionist state was now controlled by anti-Zionists.

American Demographics

All this was happening on the background of profound demographic changes in the United States. American public opinion regarding the 2014 war in Gaza (Operation Protective Edge) should have been instructive. In aggregate, American public opinion was overwhelmingly supportive of Israel and this provided tailwind to the macho posturing of the Israeli right-wing. Yet breaking this 'support' down into its demographic constituents revealed a much more ominous picture. Americans over 65 supported Israel by a margin of 24 points while those under 30 opposed Israel by a 26 point margin. White Americans supported Israel by a margin of 16 points while non-whites opposed Israel by a margin of 24 points. Every year following the percentage of older whites in the US population declined while the percentage of minorities and those born in the 1980s increased. In 2012, over 50% of children born were from non-white populations (Black, Hispanic, Asian etc.). In the same year, the Census Bureau forecast that non-Hispanic whites would become a minority in 2043 and that by 2060 would only comprise 43% of the population. In other words, those predisposed to support Israel declined in influence and those predisposed to oppose Israel increased. This eventually began to reflect itself in Congressional support for Israel which gradually began to become more similar to European attitudes. By 2014, Israel was living off its shrinking PR capital and creating little PR added value.

Chapter Twenty One

The Moral Turning Point

But more significant was the moral turning point within the Jewish population. Young secular Jews began avoiding army service and reserves as the national religious and settlers increasingly became prominent in the officer corps. The best and the brightest began to leave the country[81]. As one grandson of one of the founders of the state put it in 2017:

> My grandfather suffered much greater material hardship and danger than I ever have. But he did it in the service of a transcendent idea being translated into a concrete reality. Life in Israel has become second-rate, not in the service of a transcendent idea but because billions have gone to the settlers, billions have gone to the Haredim, billions have been wasted because of the stranglehold of the tycoons on the economy, and billions have been wasted because of monopoly workers' committees at the

ports and Electric Company. Israelis have to work three times as long for an apartment than people in Sweden and twice as long as people in the United States. Our leaders have no moral or intellectual authority yet lecture us in an arrogant manner. My private life is dictated to by a mafia of ignorant, corrupt and racist rabbis. There is more discrimination against non-Orthodox Jews in Israel than in any other country in the world. Why should I sacrifice my life for such a situation?

The erosion of Israel's moral stature and moral self-confidence because of the settlers and various religious leaders began to weigh on many young cosmopolitan Israelis who were growing more and more embarrassed by the level of public discourse and behavior in the country. The moral bankruptcy of Israel's Orthodox Rabbinate had become especially apparent. This was encapsulated in the disgraceful episode when over 40 of Israel's most prominent rabbis signed a *Halachic* judgment (Jewish analog to the Muslim *Fatwa*) that Jews should not rent homes in Israel to non-Jews. The reasons given were the danger of intermarriage and the lowering of real estate prices and that non-Jews have a "different lifestyle from Jews" which can actually endanger lives. They instructed their followers that if a Jew sells or rents property to a non-Jew, his neighbors must warn him, and if he does not change his ways, the neighbors must avoid the person, and may not conduct business with him. A person who rents or sells to non-Jews may also not be allowed to read the Torah Portion in synagogue.

Rabbi Dov Lior, the chief rabbi of Hebron and head of the *Council of Rabbis of Judea and Samaria*, was a particular egregious example of this moral erosion. As head of the *Kiryat Arba Hesder* Yeshiva which combined Talmudic studies with military service, Lior was in a position to influence the behavior of religious soldiers. He also was frequently invited by the IDF to lecture troops in the field, where he spread his views. His views included endorsing a book that advocated the killing of Palestinian children because they would grow up to kill Jews anyway; that Jewish women should not use sperm donated by a non-Jewish man since the resultant baby would have the "negative genetic traits that characterize non-Jews" because "Gentile sperm leads to barbaric offspring". He advocated using captured Arab terrorists for medical experiments (much as the Nazis used the Jews). He said it was forbidden by Jewish law to even employ Arabs. He called Barack Obama the *Kushi*[82] of the West and likened him to the genocidal enemy of the Jews, Haman, from the Book of Esther.

Lior made rabbinic rulings that labeled Yitzhak Rabin a traitor who endangered Jewish lives (rulings that under Jewish law warranted the death penalty). In fact Lior was a rabbinic advisor to Rabin's assassin Yigal Amir as well as to Baruch Goldstein, the murderer of 29 Arab worshippers at the Cave of the Patriarchs. Lior described Goldstein as "holier than all the martyrs of the Holocaust" and "Since Goldstein did what he did in God's name, he is to be regarded as a righteous man." When Lior was arrested by Israeli police on suspicion of inciting violence, demonstrations by religious supporters erupted in Jerusalem. Israel's chief rabbis condemned the arrest as a "grave offense to an important Rabbi's honor," and 25 members of Knesset signed a petition denouncing it as "shameful". Lior's salary was paid by the state as all Rabbis in Israel were state employees and his Yeshiva was financed by the state. Having it both ways (as was the wont of the radical Right of the period) he defended his right to free speech but condemned Democracy as the new idol worship of the times.

After the Goldstein massacre, Rabbi Moshe Levinger (also employed by the state) said that he was sorry for the 29 Palestinians murdered by Goldstein in the same way that he would be sorry for the killing of 29 flies. There was a huge public funeral for Goldstein, and Jewish children wore buttons with the slogan "Dr. Goldstein cured Israel's ills." At the funeral, Rabbi Israel Ariel (another state employee) eulogized him thus: "The holy martyr, Baruch Goldstein, is from now on our intercessor in heaven. Goldstein did not act as an individual; he heard the cry of the land of Israel, which is being stolen from us day after day by the Muslims. He acted to relieve that cry of the land."

Former Chief Rabbi Ovadia Yosef's various racist utterances
were not only a cause of tremendous embarrassment, but
were indicative of the moral level of Israeli society by the first
decades of the 21st century. Following are some examples:[83]

"There was a tsunami and there are terrible natural
disasters, because there isn't enough Torah study... Black
people reside there [New Orleans]. Blacks will study the
Torah? [God said] let's bring a tsunami and drown them.
Hundreds of thousands remained homeless. Tens of
thousands have been killed. All of this because they have
no God. Bush was behind Gush Katif [the Gaza settlement
bloc]. He encouraged Sharon to expel Gush Katif... We
had 15,000 people expelled here and there [New Orleans]
150,000. It was God's retribution... God does not short-
change anyone."

"Goyim were born only to serve us. Without that, they
have no place in the world – only to serve the People of
Israel." "In Israel, death has no dominion over them... With
gentiles, it will be like any person – they need to die, but
[God] will give them longevity. Why? Imagine that one's
donkey would die, they'd lose their money. "This is his
servant... That's why he gets a long life, to work well for
this Jew." "Why are Gentiles needed? They will work, they
will plow, and they will reap. We will sit like an effendi and
eat... That is why Gentiles were created."

"If a Gentile were to get injured in a car accident during
Sabbath, and he is brought to the hospital – Israel must

not treat him ... as the Torah forbids to violate the Sabbath for Gentiles ... all religious physicians who treat Gentiles on the Sabbath are violating the Sabbath"[84]

The book Torah Ha'Melech, by Rabbi Yitzchak Shapiro and Rabbi Yosef Elizur (the book Rabbi Dov Lior had famously endorsed) contained the following:

1. "In any situation in which a non-Jew's presence endangers Jewish lives, the non-Jew may be killed *even* if he is a righteous Gentile and not at all guilty for the situation that has been created".

2. There is justification for killing babies if it is clear that they will grow up to harm us, and in such a situation they (the babies) may be harmed *deliberately* and *not only* during combat with adults.

3. "... anyone who weakens our state by word or similar action is considered a pursuer" (author's note: according to Halachic law a 'pursuer' must be killed – this was the religious justification for killing Rabin; this ruling is a justification for killing left of center Israelis)

4. "In religious law, we have found that non-Jews are generally suspected of shedding Jewish blood, and in war this suspicion becomes a great deal stronger. One must consider killing even babies, who have not violated the seven Noahide laws, because of the future danger that will be caused if they are allowed to grow up to be as wicked as their parents."

One sarcastic blogger reversed the philosophy of theses Rabbis and wrote: "In any situation in which the existence of a Jew threatens the life or safety of a non-Jew, the Jew may, and should, be killed. Non-Jewish lives are too important to tolerate the danger posed by Jews".

An Israeli Orthodox "family magazine," *Fountains of Salvation* "Ma'ayanei Hayeshua" (associated with Chabad) published an article on December 25, 2010 attacking rabbis who condemned a letter circulated by pro-settler extremist rabbis urging Israeli Jews not to rent apartments to Israeli Palestinians. It chided them for being "politically correct" and refusing to do their jobs; to educate the general population in the true path of Torah which is summed up in the final sentence of the article: "It will be interesting to see whether they leave the congregating of the *Amalekites into extermination camps* (italics mine) to others, or whether they will declare that wiping out *Amalek* is no longer relevant. Only time will tell."

While the Palestinians were not explicitly named, it was clear this was what was meant. Identifying the Palestinians with Amalek had been a long tradition in settler and Gush Emunim circles. In 1980, for example, *Bat Kol*, the student publication of Bar-Ilan University (founded by and identified with modern Orthodox Jewry), published an article by Rabbi Israel Hess entitled *Genocide: A Commandment of the Torah,* which argued that the Palestinians were to Jews what darkness was to light and deserved the same fate as the

Amalekites (i.e. extermination). The president of Bar-Ilan, Rabbi Emanuel Rackman, dismissed Hess from his position at the university as a result, but Hess's article continued to be a source of intellectual inspiration for many in the settlement movement who, on a daily basis referred to the Palestinians as Amalek.

These views had an impact on religious soldiers serving in the field and in effect neutralized specific IDF codes of ethics, policies and explicit orders. Indeed, religious soldiers often consulted with Rabbis before deciding to obey or disobey IDF orders. This philosophy was deeply embedded within the social structure of the IDF itself. For example in 2009, Brig. Gen. Avichai Rontzki, Chief Rabbi of the Israel Defense Forces and a resident of the West Bank settlement of *Itamar*, told pre-army students at a settlement Yeshiva that soldiers that show mercy to the enemy will be damned. In other words a senior Israeli officer was preaching in favor of a frame of mind that was in complete contravention to the official ethical code of the IDF. Many of these extremist rabbis were invited by the Army Education Corps to lecture to soldiers in the field. Because of these phenomena, a growing number of non-religious men and women were avoiding army service; many of those who did serve refused offers to attend officer training school.

This phenomenon was not without its religious critics (including rabbis and prominent religious figures). But racist Rabbis had become the public face of Orthodox Judaism in

Israel and disgusted the best and the brightest of Israel's young more secular Jews. When they saw tycoons and politicians groveling before these fanatic rabbis they asked why should I sacrifice my life for such a society?

The stage was set for the next turning point.

Chapter Twenty Two

The Political Turning Point

The Palestinians changed their political grand strategy soon after 2020, when the first generation of Palestinian leaders not born before the establishment of Israel or before the 1967 war took control of the Palestinian National movement. Following their success in the Jerusalem elections in 2018, their next major step occurred in 2027 (60 years after the 6-Day War). The new president of the PA went before the UN and *demanded* that Israel annex the West Bank and Gaza; granting its residents full citizenship. Using a very shrewd strategy of the indirect approach he quoted Herzl, Jabotinsky and Ben Gurion as well as the Israeli Declaration of Independence and chastised the Israeli government that if they did not grant the Arabs full citizenship they would be violating the values and principles of the founding fathers of Zionism and their own declared Zionist worldview. The implicit dilemma had become explicit – *become* an Apartheid state or give up the idea of a Jewish state.

The Palestinian president's speech before the United Nations shocked the world with its pro-Zionist implications. By quoting the founding fathers and the founding document of Israel, the speech completely contravened the previous accusations of apartheid, yet in fact placed the Jewish state in a position whereby it had to either choose Apartheid or die as a Jewish state. His speech included the following quotations:

He quoted the Bible:
"Ye shall have one law, both for the stranger and for him that was born in the land" - Numbers 9:14

He quoted Israel's Declaration of Independence

1. "THE STATE OF ISRAEL … will promote the development of the country **for the benefit of all its inhabitants**; will be based on the precepts of liberty, justice and peace as envisaged by the prophets of Israel; **will uphold the full social and political equality of all its citizens, without distinction of race, creed or sex;** will guarantee full freedom of conscience, worship, education and culture; will safeguard the sanctity and inviolability of the shrines and Holy Places of all religions; and will dedicate itself to the principles of the Charter of the United Nations."

2. "WE APPEAL … to the Arab inhabitants of the State

of Israel to...play their part in the upbuilding of the State, **on the basis of full and equal citizenship** and due representation in all its bodies and institutions - provisional or permanent."

He referred to Herzl's futurist novel *Old-New-Land* in which Herzl perceived the future Jewish state as based on equal rights for all its citizens (including the right to vote), regardless of religion, race or gender. Herzl had envisioned a state that would be both Jewish and democratic, both a Jewish nation state and a state of all its citizens. This of course assumed an organic Jewish majority which would have been compromised by annexing the territories. He quoted from Herzl's diary: "I have charged the Jewish people; fashion your state in such a manner that the stranger will feel comfortable among you".

He referred to Jabotinsky's draft constitution for the future Jewish state written in 1934 which declared that Arabs would be on an equal footing with their Jewish counterparts "throughout all sectors of the country's public life." They would share the state's duties, both military and civil service, and enjoy its prerogatives. Jabotinsky proposed that Hebrew and Arabic should enjoy equal rights (including cultural rights; that Arabic should have equal standing with Hebrew) and that "in every cabinet where the prime minister is a Jew, the vice-premiership shall be offered to an Arab and *vice versa* (italics mine." He quoted Ben Gurion:"An Arab has also the right to be elected president of the state, should he be elected by all".

The quandary was unfathomable for Israel's leaders and Israel's Jewish citizens. It was as if they were caught by complete surprise. Yet, if they just had been following Palestinian social media, let alone more serious research from Israel's own intelligence agencies, they should have been expecting it. Sixty years of Israeli occupation and settlement without the creation of a separate Palestinian state had done the job. The Palestinians finally realized they were never going to get a state of their own; that there would never be a *collective* Palestinian autonomy. This realization exacerbated the desire for *individual* autonomy and self-fulfillment amongst entire generations that had matured in an era of globalization; an era whose media had highlighted the possibilities of material comfort as well as individual choice and self-realization, yet in which their own individual potential had been stunted by the occupation.

Political Israel responded with panic – Israeli citizens with angst. The chickens had come home to roost. Some right-wingers responded that Israel should annex the territories but not the population; others suggested putting the Palestinians into autonomous 'reservations' where they could rule themselves (as long as they obeyed Israel's rules). This 'Bantustan' proposal had originally been put forward as early as 2013 (but had received no serious consideration at the time) by Dr. Steven Plaut, an American Jew (graduate of Princeton) who lectured at the University of Haifa. In an article entitled "Time to Annex Judea and Samaria"[85] he proposed, amongst other things, the following:

- "Palestinian" Arabs living in the West Bank will not receive Israeli citizenship and will not vote in Israeli national elections.

- "Palestinians" choosing to remain in the West Bank will live in reservations, in some ways resembling Native-American-Indian territories that function inside the United States (possibly even including casinos), although in some ways they will differ. Reservations will be operated in those parts of the West Bank that have large concentrations of Arab population, meaning Jericho, Nablus, Ramallah, Jenin, Tul Karem, and a few other areas. Reservations will NOT have territorial contiguity.

This provoked a firestorm of international and Jewish criticism as actually confirming earlier charges of apartheid. Both the EU *and* the USA warned Israel that if these suggestions were carried out, all diplomatic and economic relations would be severed. This had become politically possible because the demographically diluted pro-Israel lobby in the USA had become greatly weakened over the previous 15 years.

The Diminishing of Diaspora Power

Again, demographics were a major cause of this diminishment. From 2% of the American population, Jews had fallen to a little

over 1%. As noted above, Americans of European extraction
had fallen to less than 50% of the population and the majority
of Americans were Black, Hispanic, Asian or other groups
of color. The Muslim population of the United States had
long since outstripped the Jewish population and they had
become increasingly organized and politically active. It had
been 82 years since the end of WWII and very few people were
alive who had been adults during the Holocaust and in any
case it had not been the crime of the majority of Americans'
ancestors. The last murderer and last survivor had long since
died. It was still remembered as an historical event but by
2027, carried little actual political weight.

The 2012 presidential elections had been the Jewish turning
point. They revealed not only that one did not have to support
the policies of the Likud to get the Jewish vote, but that
Israel was no longer a primary factor with the Jewish vote.
Despite unconcealed support for Romney by Israel's Prime
Minister and much of American Jewish leadership, as well
as ferocious attacks on Obama on the Jewish blogosphere
69% of American Jewry still voted for Obama. This was down
from the 78% that had voted for Obama in 2008 but was still
the fourth largest percentage of other ethnic groups – after
African-Americans, Hispanics and Asians. The canard that
Jewish Americans were single-issue voters whose support
went to those candidates with the most hawkish views on
Israel was proven to be false. 82% of American Jews supported
a two-state solution and 76% wanted President Obama to

put forward a peace plan. In other words, if American Jews could have voted in Israel, a pro-compromise center-left coalition would have ruled Israel and not a Likud-dominated right-wing government. Unfortunately the majority was nowhere near the involvement with Israel as the radical Jewish right-wing.

Large numbers of American Jews, especially amongst the younger demographics, were greatly annoyed with and even embarrassed in particular by the positions and behaviors of the Netanyahu government. Right-wing macho posturing had very little impact on them. Many of the more politically informed were mortified by the level of religious discourse in Israel as exemplified in the previous chapter. The fact that so many of Israel's political and business leaders sucked up to racist rabbis rather than condemning them simply increased Jewish alienation from Israel and the Zionist idea. The fact that most mainstream American Jewish leaders did not even condemn this ugly phenomenon increased their alienation from the organized Jewish community and eventually, by extension, from Jewish identity itself. In the November 5, 2013 edition of *The Tablet* magazine, Jewish American intellectual Dr. Adam Garfinkle brilliantly detailed the erosion of American Jewish power in an article entitled "The Broken Triangle" (referring to Israel, America and American Jewry). It was irrefutable in its analysis of a rapidly changing state of affairs that was corroding the special relationship between Israel and American Jewry, and between Israel and America.[86]

In the 2012 Presidential elections, the overwhelming majority of American Jewish voters viewed the economy, not Israel, as their top electoral concern. This was followed by health care, Social Security and Medicare. In 2012, it turned out that Jewish Americans had the same voting concerns as most other Americans. This internal Jewish reality of declining political punch and automatic identification with Israel met a growing public disgust with all things associated with Middle East, including Israel. The Iraq and Afghanistan wars had been the longest in American history and after Vietnam the most unpopular – especially when, as soon as the American troops left, both countries reverted to internecine savagery. The four trillion dollars and tens of thousands of lives the Americans had spent on both wars were seen as a colossal waste of blood and treasure. Moreover, by 2018 new energy technologies and oil drilling techniques had enabled the United States to become independent of Mid East oil and by 2020 from all OPEC oil. NAFTA had become oil self-sufficient and as a consequence, the United States removed its entire military presence in the Persian Gulf by 2020.

The Israel-Arab conflict was the one area the Americans had remained involved in – mainly due to American Jewish and Evangelical support for Israel. But the decline in the political clout of both groups, joined with the disgust with all things associated with Middle East had begun to erode the American political preoccupation with Israel. Following 2020, American public opinion had begun to be increasingly disgusted with the never ending Israeli-Palestinian conflict. Many felt that the PA president's speech only sanctioned what had become a reality on the ground and was a good way to get rid of the whole problem as an American political obsession.

Immediately following the Palestinian President's speech, the Zionist center-left put forth the two-state solution again and many in the Right, in desperation, agreed to it; but it was too late. The Palestinians turned it down (sarcastically: "it seems we have become more Zionist than the Jews"). Half a million Israeli settlers in West Bank violently demonstrated against the two-state solution. Nationalist religious officers (now the majority of the officer corps in the IDF) discretely let Israel's leaders know that they would refuse any order in response to a two-state solution – a de facto putsch of Israeli policy-making. The Israeli government fell and new elections were held.

New Palestinian Tactics

The new Palestinian strategy had quickly been reduced to very effective tactics. Previously, after the 2017 municipal elections, Palestinian leaders encouraged ever increasing numbers of East Jerusalemites to petition for and receive Israeli citizenship. By 2020, a large number were eligible

to vote in national elections as well as municipal ones. The
Arab citizens of Israel abjured their previously indifferent
attitude to general elections in which hardly 50% of eligible
voters did vote. Arab voter participation had increased from
50% in 2012 to 90% in 2027 and 20 Arab MKs were now in
the Knesset. One of the causes was the rise of electoral
threshold in 2014 from 2% to 3.25% which was intended to
drive the three small Arab parties out of the Knesset, in effect
disenfranchising the Arab minority, but which in effect had
the opposite effect – it galvanized the Arab street from its
electoral apathy and participation increased dramatically.
The law of unintended consequences had prevailed.

The Palestinians in the West Bank and Gaza had petitioned
for the right to vote but of course had been denied – a tactic
that in itself had become a great PR victory for them. But
they trumped that PR success on Election Day itself. They
set up faux voting stations and invited outside observers to
oversee their faux elections in the territories. These observers
included senior retired European judges, Nobel Prize winners,
prominent artistic and media celebrities as well as several
former Prime Ministers of major European countries. The
international media was out in force for this staged media
event. So that when Israel denied entry to several of these
people it became a major PR catastrophe for Israel. The
even bigger PR catastrophe was on Election Day, when the
Israeli army moved in on these voting stations, arrested
the supervisors and aggressively dispersed the people

lined up to vote, injuring some of the foreign observers. Headlines around the world were variations on "The Day Israel's Democracy Died". The international criticism was total, absolute and crushing. Even the United States and Germany were unrestrained in their criticism. Israel had become completely isolated.

Major international as well as home-grown companies in knowledge intensive sectors (IT, pharmaceuticals, clean-tech etc.) began moving out of Israel – a process that had begun with the increased emigration of Israel's best and brightest. Secular hi-tech Israel effectively went on strike. The *Startup Nation* of the 1990s and first decade of the 21st century was as much a result of a cultural attitude and educational infrastructure that had been inherited from the pioneering era as it was of a liberalized economic policy. The irony was that just as the *Startup Nation* began to flourish in the 1990s, the erosion of the educational infrastructure and the cultural self-confidence that had made it possible had begun.

Lincoln had said that "A house divided against itself cannot stand ... (a) government cannot endure, permanently, half slave and half free ... It will become all one thing or all the other." This had become an analogy for Israel's post 1967 political and cultural struggle – it had become "a house divided against itself"; it had become half globalized, cosmopolitan hi-tech and half ultra-nationalist, theocratic back to the biblical past. These two halves could not for long live together in peace. Israel had to become one thing or the other. Since the globalized half had no coherent ideology that characterized them as a political force and the settler half did, Israel had long been on the road to becoming the settler half. Moreover, a substantial number of people who were in the first half sociologically often had ideological and political sympathy with the other half. Some commentators had observed that Israel's political class began to display signs of a nervous breakdown. Others owned that their irrational behavior in the name of national 'honor' simply demonstrated that Israel had indeed become part of the Middle East – sacrificing the vital historic national interest to the vague concept of Israel's 'honor'

Within five years, by 2032, the Arab MKs (now 25 in number) had established extensive log-rolling agreements which constituted a de facto coalition with Haredim. They automatically voted for every bit of religious and welfare legislation that the Haredim proposed, as long as the Haredim supported every bit of development and education proposals of the Arabs. As a result, Israel became more and more theocratic and more and more suffocating for young non-Orthodox Jewry, and the exodus of young talented Jews from Israel increased apace. Fifty percent of Israel's population was now Arab or Haredi, and 45 of the Knesset members were now identified with one or other group. Add on the part of Israel that identified with the National Religious, and less than 40% of Israel's population could be identified with liberal western constitutionalist principles. The de facto Arab-Haredi coalition eased the claims for Israeli citizenship for Arabs in the territories. In 2032, Silicon Wadi – Start-up Nation – had ceased to exist. The exodus of the best and the brightest had gutted Israel's defense and intelligence capabilities. The long slide to the end had begun. By 2038, the majority of Members of Knesset were Arab or Haredi and by 2046 the majority was Arab. A bill was introduced to change the name of the country to Palestine. By 2048, the country known as Israel had ceased to exist, 100 years after its establishment.

Conclusion:

What Could Have Been: *Rational Grand Strategy*

"Politics is the sense of smell, to predict what can – and what cannot – be achieved. One should demand only that which can be achieved."

Chaim Weizmann

Grand Strategy refers to the nexus and proper use of the economic, professional, intellectual, social, cultural, scientific and moral resources of a nation. These resources are the fundamental foundations of all military power – especially in democratic societies and especially in the post-industrial, globalized 21st century reality. B. H. Liddell Hart, the renowned British military philosopher, in his classic book *Strategy*, endowed the predominance of "grand strategic resources" – and its association with a "policy of limited aims" and the "strategy of the indirect approach" – with overriding policy making status. Some of his *tactical* disciples included German generals Rommel and Guderian, and American general George Patton. His views (directly and indirectly) greatly influenced the operational philosophy of the early Israel Defense Forces. Israeli generals who acknowledged his influence in regards to the "strategy of the indirect approach" included Yigal Yadin, Yigal Allon, Haim Laskov and Yitzhak Rabin.

Unfortunately Liddell Hart's impact on Israeli political policy-making was negligible – only Ben Gurion and Weizmann intuitively understood the "policy of limited aims" as reflected in the constraints on "grand strategic resources". Ben Gurion's dispute with Israel's second Chief of Staff, Yigal Yadin, highlighted the chasm between those who thought tactically and strategically versus those that thought grand strategically. Yadin became Chief of Staff of the IDF in November 1949 and served for three years. He resigned in December 1952, over disagreements with Prime Minister David Ben Gurion about cuts in the military budget. Yadin wanted the defense budget to be one third of the national budget. Ben Gurion wanted to cut it in order to invest massively in education and infrastructure development. He was reported to have argued "what good is it if I buy you tanks but the crew is technologically illiterate; all you will really have is a lot of expensive junk".

Like Weizmann, Liddell Hart believed that responsible leaders should adapt their aim to circumstances, or develop new means to make the aim more possible, or to invent new aims. In other words, one's aims should reflect one's grand strategic resources and one must always devote one's energies to increasing those resources. Wasting grand strategic resources on unachievable ideological aims and military adventures is a recipe for economic and political disaster. The American experience in Vietnam, Afghanistan and Iraq and its disastrous economic consequences that caused severe damage to America's social fabric, is proof of this.

Liddell Hart's philosophy molded the operational principles of the Israeli Army in its early days, but had little influence on Israel's political leaders when it came to policy-making following the 6-Day War. This may explain why Israel's early military operations were usually more successful than its political policies and why later military operations dedicated to absolutist ("once and for all") aims such as the Lebanese War and the so called "War on Terror" were markedly unsuccessful.

There is no question that Israel had serious tactical and strategic problems associated with returning territories conquered in the 6-Day War. These fears were real and substantive. The problem was that the grand strategic threat of not giving them back was much more profound. The strategic and tactical threats could have been handled. The grand strategic threat could not, and it was the grand strategic threat that finally destroyed Israel. Demographics (internal and external), erosion of moral self-confidence, loss of world sympathy, debilitation of economic robustness, decline of the education system – all in aggregate deriving from a blind ideological devotion to land idolatry, finally destroyed the Zionist project.

If the Zionist leaders of the 21st century had fully understood the benefits of a policy of limited aims, the State of Israel would still be a vibrant member of the community of nations and perhaps even be a beacon of light to human civilization in general. The Talmudic warning that "he who tries to get everything ends up with nothing" (*Tafasta merubeh, lo tafasta*) had become a self-fulfilling prophecy.

Epilogue

By 'defeating' the Jews, the Palestinians destroyed themselves. No one in the world cared about "The Palestinian Problem" anymore. The Palestine that emerged from the rubble of the self-destroyed Israel was without natural resources and without human resources. Every Jew that was able had fled to the West – those that could were those that had human resource value to the West. Silicon Wadi (Start-up Nation) simply got on a plane and relocated to wherever they were so inclined. Doctors, nurses, engineers and scientists followed suit. The Technion and Weizmann Institute were 'purchased' by large second-tier research universities in the American heartland which immediately elevated these universities into first-tier elite status. All the hard Science and Mathematics departments of Israel's research universities were bought up by various other academic institutions in the United States. Many other academics (especially in the Humanities and Social Sciences) relocated individually – some to second- and third-tier academic institutions, and others to teach middle and high school. Israeli water experts (scientists, engineers, and entrepreneurs) were welcome in every arid zone country in the world.

Subsequently, the emerging body of Palestinian scientists and engineers found little opportunity (creative or livelihood) in this barren new Palestine and joined their Jewish colleagues in this exodus. Palestinian secular intelligentsia – doctors, lawyers etc. – found the theocratic atmosphere of the new Palestine choking. Educated secular Palestinian women could not wait to escape the cultural prison of patriarchal Islam. All Christian minorities – educated or not – fled the country within five years after the creation of Palestine. The maximalist Palestine that had emerged on the entire land of Israel emerged as a failed state. The suicide of the Jews was also the death knell of the Palestinian National Movement.

Jews who could not flee formed themselves into a variety of self-defense militias. The various Palestinian factions began slaughtering one another and pitched battles between the Jewish militias and Palestinian factions were a daily occurrence. Palestine became a failed state like Somalia. This was a situation intolerable to neighboring countries. What was left of the Syrian army invaded the Galilee; the Egyptians occupied the rest of the country. Syria annexed Lebanon and Jordan, and what had been Tel Aviv became the new border between Egypt and Syria. The world did not intervene, and did not care and there were no mass protests against the slaughter – after all it was Arab slaughtering Arab, not Jews defending themselves against Jihadists. Europe and the US assuaged their consciences by allowing hordes of Jewish and Christian refugees to find refuge in their countries.

Diaspora Jewish communities and organized Jewish life collapsed and all but the ultra-Orthodox quickly assimilated (including the national religious who now had no raison d'être for existing without the Land of Israel). The Haredim survived as an anthropological curiosity much like the Amish. The Jewish people vanished from the earth as a historical force.

Appendix

Defining Our Terms

<u>Ideology</u> – *1) the body of* doctrine, *myth, symbol etc. of a social movement, institution, class or group; 2) such a body of* doctrine...*with reference to some political or cultural plan.* *
<u>Policy</u> – *1) a definite course of action adopted for the sake of expediency and facility, 2) actions or procedures conforming to or considered with reference to prudence or expediency.** This means the conversion of ideological doctrine into concrete, understandable and *achievable* goals. Achievable is the key word, because, as Liddell Hart (and Weizmann) pointed out, available resources and general political and economic context always constrain plans. Hence their advocacy for policies of limited aims. Policy might be prescribed by ideology but grand strategic limitations must define concrete policy aims. Therefore an ideology of a "Greater Israel" on the part of the Jews or a "Greater Palestine" on the part of the Palestinians could never have succeeded. The attempt

to achieve such goals entailed a profound waste of resources and energy and eventually destroyed the national project of both nations.

Grand Strategy – *The aggregate of the economic, political, military, social and moral resources of a people and how best to optimally mobilize them in order minimize weaknesses and optimize strengths in order to achieve vital goals.* Grand Strategy defines criteria and priorities, in determining policy goals; it is the filter through which we pass our policy goals to see if they are appropriate. In a rational entity Grand Strategy should determine policy *more than ideology.* Ideology might define an ideal outcome but policies must be based upon realistic evaluations of the political principle of the art of the possible. Grand Strategy is the keystone of any policy.

Strategy – *1) a plan, method or series of maneuvers or stratagems for obtaining a specific goal or event, 2) the applied planning and mobilization of grand strategic resources vis-à-vis one's policy aims. Strategy mobilizes resources, forms alliances and makes specific plans for implementation.* *

Tactics – *1) adroit maneuvering, technique or procedure for gaining advantage or success, 2) tactics are the means by which strategic aims are pursued in specific situations or in regards to specific aspects of the overall strategy.* *[87]

SWOT/PEST Analysis – *The candid evaluation of strengths, weaknesses, opportunities and threats within a global political, economic, social and technological environment that a people (or organization) must deal with;* an honest SWOT/PEST analysis is a vital part of grand strategic thinking. It defines the art of the possible and thus becomes the basis for a policy of limited aims. It also indicates how one might formulate various strategies and tactics of the indirect approach.

Grand Strategy and the Question of Values

Coherent Grand Strategies must distinguish between primary values, secondary values and periodic values in order to quiet maximalist ideologues. Primary values are values that are universal in time and place. Secondary values are values that serve primary values, optimizing their chance of fulfillment. Periodic values are values vital for assuring primary and secondary values within a particular historical environment and context.

Examples of primary values would be freedom, dignity, justice and equality before the law – values that are *inherently* valuable. Examples of secondary values would be equality of access to education and diminishing inequalities in income as major instruments for guaranteeing optimal justice and equality before the law. This recognizes that in a free society poverty restricts freedom of choice in practice, while discrepancies in education and standards of living almost guarantee non-equality before the law. This is not only a moral question, it has grand strategic implications. The aggregate power of a nation ultimately depends on the extent its citizens feel a part of the national project and not being taken advantage of by the "national" project.

Military power is ultimately dependent on the *quality* of a country's soldiers no matter its technological and weapons system superiority; the ability to extend its military presence over time is dependent on its economic robustness; its economic robustness is dependent on the productivity of its citizens; productivity is a product of education which optimizes the abilities of the individual, which ultimately depends on standard of living. Willingness to sacrifice for the general good depends on identification with organized society; identification with organized society is a function of not feeling screwed by the system. Any policy dependent on driving wages down and widening income gaps is therefore ultimately unpatriotic.

Income equality is *not* a primary value; it is not inherently valuable in and of itself *unless* it serves freedom, justice and equality before the law. If income equality was inherently valuable Pol Pot's Cambodia and Taliban's Afghanistan would have been moral entities, characterized by radical equality in standards of living; i.e. *everyone* at the same abysmal level of poverty and deprivation of fundamental human rights. Also the Jim Crow south would have been the most moral region in the United States – given that the income difference between white and black sharecroppers was marginal and there were very few super rich. Equality is without moral standing unless it serves primary values.

Periodic values refer to specific programs or practices or rules that are established in a certain historical period in support of secondary and primary values, but which might over time become dysfunctional to the very secondary and primary values they were originally designed to serve. In a general context this might refer to certain aspects, programs and social service delivery systems of a welfare state. In a particular period they might have reinforced equality and sustained human freedom and dignity but in another period they might perpetuate poverty, creating dependence and manipulative obsequiousness on the part of the welfare recipient. There is no question, for example, that the public education systems developed in the West and copied around the world had a tremendous if not predominant impact on raising the civilizational level of the human race over the course of 150 years, especially as it answered the needs of the industrial age. But by the late 20th century, when the human race was moving from the industrial to the technological age, serious flaws in public education systems based on the factory/ assembly line paradigm were becoming apparent. Yet many educators out of self-interest and nostalgia kept advocating that the system itself was a value and that radically rethinking the ways that education was delivered was somehow against education and against the educators.

In the Zionist context, the collective and cooperative settlement projects (Kibbutz and Moshav) that characterized so much of the heroic period of the Zionist enterprise might be termed periodic values. These entities were of value because they were a vital component in the fight for the primary values of Jewish independence and freedom. They functioned in a highly egalitarian way thus guaranteeing high morale. In other words during a particular historical period these settlements manifested important secondary values that were vital for sustaining primary values. But when these settlements became just another place where people live, making no special contribution to national independence or individual freedom, their most talented members leaving, then of what special value were they in the 21st century? Related periodic values such as 'the conquest of the land' and the 'conquest of the labor market' became less relevant and eventually racist in the post state reality. Labor Zionists did not understand this paradigm change. This lack of historical awareness, in conjunction with radical demographic changes (the political empowerment of religiously observant Middle Eastern Jews and the immigration of over a million Jews from the former Soviet Union) as well as economic globalization, led to the Zionist left's descent into political irrelevance.

The price Israel paid for being rooted in and infatuated by the periodic successes of the past, was the loss of grand strategic focus. The consequence was the pursuit of self-defeating and dysfunctional policies, which reflected confusion between primary values, secondary values and periodic values. Examples of this lack of grand strategic focus were abundant and explained the gap between Israel's security, social, economic, political, democratic and ecological situation and the expectations and desires of most of Israel's citizens in the decades of its decline.

Endnotes

1 *International New York Times* Sept. 10, 2014, pg 12 in review by Steven Aschheim of *Eichmann Before Jerusalem* by Bettina Stangneth, Alfred A. Knopf 2014

2 Cochran, Gregory and Harpending, Henry. *10,000 Year Explosion,* New York, Basic Books (2009)

3 Pellissier ,Hank . *Why is the IQ of Ashkenazi Jews so High?*; Illinois, Wilcox Publishing (2012)

4 This was essentially a return to a more biblical identity. The words Jewish Religion do not appear even once in the Bible while the term Nation of Israel or People of Israel or Children of Israel appear scores of times.

5 Eliot, T.S. *After Strange Gods*, New York; Harcourt, Brace and Co; 1st edition (1934) pg 19

6 *Bills of Attainder* are laws especially designed to impose legal sanctions or disabilities on a particular individual or

class of people. They have been unconstitutional in the Anglo Saxon legal tradition since the Magna Carta and are specifically banned in the English Bill of Rights and in the American Constitution.

7 Sjølyst-Jackson, Peter. *Troubling legacies: migration, modernism and fascism in the case of Knut Hamsun.* 2010: Continuum International Publishing Group; p. 16.

8 Holden, Stephen. "From His Olympian Heights, Deaf to the Alarm Below"; New York Times on the Web, August 6, 1997

9 Gay, Peter. *The Enlightenment: Volume II*; New York, W. W. Norton & Company, 1996. pg 92

10 Roll, Eric. *A History of Economic Thought*; Eastbourne, England, Anthony Rowe, 1992 Pg 19

11 Harold Fisch. *The Zionist Revolution*; Weidenfeld and Nicolson, London (1978), p. 79

12 Weizmann, Chaim. *Trial and Error,* Harper & Brothers Publishers, New York (1949) pgs 444-5

13 In reality the 'Inverted Pyramid' was always an ideological invention. A work of fiction, *The Brothers Ashkenazi* by I.J. Singer, presents a more realistic picture of the socio-economic structure of the Jews in Eastern Europe in the 19th and early 20th centuries – the vast majority toiled either in textile factories or as independent artisans and teamsters and were not *Luftmenschen.*

14 Sarig, Mordechai. *The Political and Social Philosophy of Ze'ev Jabotinsky: Selected Writings;* Vallentine Mitchell, London, Pg 73 (1999)

15 Speech at the founding conference of the New Zionist Organization (reflecting the Revisionist movement's political philosophy) in Vienna in 1935

16 Katz, Shmuel http//:www.israpundit.com/archives/25840 *Oct. 18, 1980 edition of the Jerusalem Post*

17 *Ma'apach* = literally the overturning: when the Likud finally replaced Labor as the ruling party of Israel since 1948 and of the entire Zionist project since 1935

18 Begin coined the phrase *"HaKol Shafit"* ('everything is judgeable') to stress the constitutional preeminence of the judicial branch over the legislative and executive branches – demonstrating a clear preference for constitutional democracy over majoritarian democracy.

19 Jabotinsky, *The Jewish War Front*, pp. 216-20 Greenwood Press (1975)

20 Quoted in *The Political Philosophy of Zionism: Trading Jewish Words for a Hebraic Land* by Eyal Chowers p.41, Cambridge University Press. New York, 2012

21 Ibid

22 Wagner, Matthew. "Who's afraid of a halachic state? Jerusalem Post.12/10/2009

23 Rabbi Jablon, Shmuel."A Halachic State According To Rav Yitzchak Isaac Halevi Herzog" *Or Shmuel* (HTC Press, 1994)

24 Laor Yitzhak. "Shtetl Equality" *Ha'Aretz* March 11, 2013

25 Rosensweig, Franz. *The Star of Redemption.* Beacon Press, Boston (1972), pg 299

26 Goitein, S.D. *Jews and Arabs: Their Contacts Through the Ages.* Schocken Books, New York (1964), pg. 99

27 Halpern, Ben. *The Idea of the Jewish* State. Harvard University Press, Cambridge, Mass. (1969)Pg.6

28 Scholem, Gershom G. *On the Kabbalah and Its Symbolism.* Schocken Books, New York (paperback edition) 4th printing (1973), pg.2 *the myth of exile and redemption* relates entirely to the land of Israel

29 Pinsker, the author of *Auto Emancipation* also did not believe that 'Zion' had to be the territory of majority Jewish autonomy. The Land of Israel was not even mentioned by him

30 Ironically one Theodore Hertza, a Gentile Viennese journalist, was lobbying for a Christian utopian community called *Freeland* in Uganda at the same time. The similarity of names, professions and geographic origins did not redound well for either initiative. The white settlers dismissed both as silly initiatives.

31 One can see the visual manifestation of this in statues on the facades of medieval cathedrals; statues that represented

the triumphant church replacing the broken synagogue (blind with broken staff).

32 Literally to restore the Jews to their homeland

33 Ken Koltun-Fromm. *Moses Hess and Modern Jewish Identity*; Indiana University Press (2001); pg 40

34 Falk, Raphael "Zionism, Race and Eugenics" *In Jewish Tradition and the Challenge of Darwinism* (edited by G. N. Cantor, Marc Swetlitz) University of Chicago Press (2006) Pg 138

35 Margolin, Ron. *The Historic Mission of Jewish Humanism and its Maskilic Origins*; abstract of paper presented at the Moses Hess Conference; Jerusalem 2012

36 http//:en.wikipedia.org/wiki/National_mysticism

37 Zionism's preoccupation with the rebirth of Hebrew was completely within the context of European Romantic nationalism's preoccupation with reinventing national languages to make them suitable for the modern era. It is impossible to imagine the emergence of Ben Yehuda in any other context.

38 Kaplan, Eran. *The Jewish Radical Right: Revisionist Zionism and Its Ideological Legacy*; University of Wisconsin Press; (2005), (p. 150).

39 Ibid pgs 8,9

40 "Pilsudski Kisses Jewish Soldier Crippled in War for Polish

Independence", *Jewish Telegraphic Agency*, (August 10, 1926)

41 Heehs, Peter, "Idea of India", http://lifepositive.com/idea-of-india/ (**April 2004)**

42 Heehs, Peter, "Religious Nationalism and Beyond", *Auroville Today* (August 2004)

43 Ibid

44 Repeated many times in his speeches

45 http://americanjewisharchives.org/journal/PDF/1976_28_01_00_schmidt.pdf

46 *Bills of Attainder: laws especially designed to impose legal sanctions or disabilities on a particular individual or class of people. They have been unconstitutional in the Anglo Saxon legal tradition since the Magna Carta and are specifically banned in the English Bill of Rights and in the American.*

47 United Nations Convention relating to the Status of Refugees Article 1(A) (2) [1951]

48 Arthur Koestler, in his book *Promise and Fulfillment* documents this in some detail.

49 http//:www.bhutaneserefugees.com/

50 http//:www.arcrelief.org/site/PageServer?pagename=learn_globalrefugeecrisis

51 http//:www.hafsite.org?/q=media/pr/discrimination-and-persecution-plight-hindus-pakistan

52 http://mideasttruth.com/forum/viewtopic.php?t=8877

53 By 2014 this figure had grown significantly.

54 Dombey, Daniel. "Turkey's Alevi minority fear future under Erdogan presidency", *Financial times*, July 27, 2014

55 http//:www.bbc.co.uk/history/british/empire_seapower/white_slaves_01.shtml

56 http//:www.city-journal.org/html/17_2_urbanities-thomas_jefferson.html

57 http//:en.wikipedia.org/wiki/Islamic_views_on_slavery#Arab_slave_trade

58 Ibid

59 Molotsky, Irvin . "Red Cross admits knowing of the holocaust during the war", *New York Times*, December 19, 1996

60 Preston , David Lee. "HITLER'S SWISS CONNECTION", *Philadelphia Inquirer*, Jan. 5, 1997

61 *Manchester Guardian*. 24 May 1939. p. 8.

62 Schmuel, More, Zvi, Yehuda. *Al-Farhud*, Magnes Press, Jerusalem, 2010

63 Finkelstein, Louis *The Jews: their history, culture, and religion*, Harper (1960). . p. 679.

64 De Haas, Jacob *History of Palestine: The Last Two Thousand Years,* MacMillan Company; First Edition (1934) p. 345.

65 Grunebaum, G.E. "Eastern Jewry Under Islam", *Viator* (1971), p. 369

66 http://www.quora.com/Was-there-anti-Semitism-in-the-Middle-East-before-Israel-and-the-rise-of-Zionism

67 Quoted in <u>*The Jews of Islam*</u>, Princeton University Press, 1984. pp. 181–183 by <u>Bernard</u> Lewis

68 Jewish Communities in Exotic Places," by Ken Blady, Jason Aronson, 2000, page 10

69 *Middle Eastern Studies* (1971), p. 232

70 Rejwan Nissim. *The Many Faces of Islam: Perspectives on a Resurgent Civilization.* <u>University Press of Florida</u>, 2000 pg11

71 <u>Letter From President Yasser Arafat to President Clinton</u>

72 Bisk, Tsvi; Dror, Moshe *Futurizing the Jews.* Praeger Press (Westport CT) 2003, pgs160-161

73 Wagner,Donald."The Evangelical-Jewish Alliance", *The Christian Century*, June 28, 2003:20-24

74 Shalev, Chemin. "AIPAC is an awe-inspiring organization, but the right-wing tilt is in its DNA; Haaretz Mar. 6, 2013

75 Weizmann, Chaim. *Trial and Error*; Harper Brothers New York (1949) pg.444

76 Mearsheimer, John J. & Walt, Stephen M. *The Israel Lobby and U.S. Foreign Policy*; Farrar, Straus and Giroux (2008)

77 Interesting to note that Hebrew has no word for subtle; hence in Israeli political culture, subtle was not even a concept

78 Koestler, Arthur. *Promise and Fulfillment.* New York, The MacMillan Company (1949) Pg.184

79 Hasson, Nir. "A surprising process of 'Israelization' is taking place among Palestinians in East Jerusalem", *Ha'aretz Magazine*, December 29, 2012

80 Hasson, Nir. "Palestinian Zionism", *Ha'aretz*, Sep. 4, 2012

81 Although as of 2014 Israel had 2nd lowest rate of emigration in west – after the United States

82 In popular Hebrew parlance of the time a racist pejorative for Black people; analogous to *Schwartza* in Yiddish

83 Berman, Lazar "Ovadia Yosef's most controversial quotations", Times of Israel, October 9, 2013

84 http://www.ynetnews.com/articles/0,7340,L-4229767,00.html

85 http//:frontpagemag.com/2013/steven-plaut/time-to-annex-judea-and-samaria-2/

86 http//:www.tabletmag.com/jewish-news-and-politics/151158/broken-triangle

87 *Random House Dictionary (College Edition)*; New York, 1968

Index with sub-headings

Printed in Great Britain
by Amazon.co.uk, Ltd.,
Marston Gate.